GLOSSARY OF
SEMIOTICS

Jo Glorie
Series General Editor
c/o Paragon House
90 Fifth Avenue
New York, N.Y. 10011

A PARAGON HOUSE GLOSSARY
FOR RESEARCH, READING, AND WRITING

GLOSSARY OF SEMIOTICS

VINCENT M. COLAPIETRO

PARAGON HOUSE

New York

First edition, 1993

Published in the United States by

Paragon House
90 Fifth Avenue
New York, N.Y. 10011

Copyright © 1993 by Paragon House

Library of Congress Cataloging-in-Publication Data

Colapietro, Vincent Michael
    Glossary of semiotics / Vincent M. Colapietro.—1st ed.
    p.   cm.—(Paragon House glossaries for research, reading,
and writing)
    Includes bibliographical references.
    ISBN 1-55778-564-3   —ISBN 1-55778-502-3
    1. Semiotics—Glossaries, vocabularies, etc.   I. Title.
II. Series.
P99.C569   1993
302.2—dc20   92-32621
                                                CIP

Manufactured in the United States of America

To Jo Glorie, who has enabled me
to bring coherence and life
to these sentences—and much more.

Contents

Acknowledgments

In composing this glossary, I learned what I should have already known. Writing even a short book is no small undertaking, especially if the book tries to cover a terrain as vast and varied as darkest semiotica. Several individuals have greatly assisted me in my efforts to map this terrain. Dominic Balestra, the chair of my department at Fordham University, has—among countless other kindnesses, large and small—provided me with the ideal research assistant: Matt Kuenning. Matt's precision, responsibility, and intelligence were invaluable. Elizabeth Vozzola has been, even in the most difficult of circumstances, insightful and encouraging, while Peter Carlo has been both an inspiring presence and a welcome distraction.

Professors Andrea Birch, Katharine Stephenson, and John K. Sheriff have offered extremely helpful comments on a draft of this work. Each has made a unique contribution to the realization of this project.

Whenever my sentences tangled, or my spirits sagged, or distractions threatened to undermine this project, my editor Jo Glorie always managed to find the *mots justes*—giving me hope that I might also. The inception of this glossary, and the series of which it is a part, reveal her editorial vision; the completion of this book reveals her editorial skill.

V.M.C.

Introduction

This glossary is designed for people who have little or no acquaintance with the field of research known as semiotics (from the Greek word *semeion*, sign). Semiotics is the general study of signs, of whatever conveys meaning. Contributors to this study have discovered much of value, but when one turns to their writings it is easy to feel frustrated and even angry at being unable to crack the code in which viewpoints are expressed and research presented. It is certainly ironic that the field of semiotics is, so frequently, a tower of Babel in which the possibility of communication and understanding is frustrated by neologisms (newly coined words) and idiosyncratic usages of ordinary terms. Hence the need for this glossary. Its goal is simply to enhance the possibilities for communication and understanding by defining the key terms of semiotic discourse in a clear and straightforward way.

The terms defined in this volume were selected on the basis of their centrality to the field of semiotics, broadly conceived. The words most often found in the indexes to books on semiotics are defined here, with no one perspective or tradition being unduly privileged. The entries vary in character, ranging from the briefest of definitions to short essays in which the reader is provided information regarding such matters as historical background or contemporary controversies. In addition, the entries are, with few exceptions, self-contained: The reader can find the basic meanings of a term in a single entry. In any given entry, references to other entries in which important collateral information can be found are identified by **boldface** type; for example, in the first entry, on abduction, one encounters **hypothesis, deduction, induction,** and **Peirce,** among others. The terms in boldface are suggestions of other terms the reader might check in order to attain a fuller understanding of the term being defined.

There is, of course, no substitute for reading widely and deeply in semiotics. Indeed, one could commit to memory all of the entries in this glossary and still be semiotically illiterate, for semiotic literacy resides, first and foremost, in the capacity to make sense out of terms in context—terms as they are used by a particular author in a particular text. But how a specific term is being used in its context is not always clear: At times neither author nor context provides us the information or insight we need to interpret what the text says. When this is so, it proves helpful to learn how the term is generally or characteristically used by various authors and, in the case of highly idiosyncratic usages, how the term is uniquely employed by an individual author. A lexicon or glossary is a compilation and, inevitably, a distillation of just such uses. It gives us something to consult when we are at a loss to know what an author means or what a text says.

The dream of attaining a comprehensive theory of signs draws upon a prior, practical acquaintance with signs. While our reflections upon signs have evolved into highly abstract definitions and theories, these reflections themselves have grown out of our most basic abilities and engagements, beginning with our ability to perceive the immediate environment and our own organic states. Signs are, without exaggeration, omnipresent: under our very noses and at our fingertips. The stench we smell tells us that something foul is near, the prick we feel that something sharp is all too near! The pangs in my stomach mean it is time to eat. In a gradual and often painful process, human infants acquire the skills to interpret a complex array of sensory clues. The mastery of such rudimentary skills makes possible more far-reaching and open-ended processes of interpretation, such as literary criticism, scientific inquiry, and philosophical reflection.

Footprints appearing on an isolated beach for the first time indicate to a marooned observer that the island is not, as previously supposed, uninhabited. The shape of a leaf imprinted on a newly exposed slab of stone turns out to be a crucial clue in discovering a species of plant long extinct. Red spots appearing one morning all over a child's body signify to all intelligent persons that something's wrong and to the trained observer that it's a case of chicken pox. A red octagon with white border and letters appearing at the end of an exit off the highway announces the necessity to stop. A president appearing on television with a minister at his side may intend to signify the righteousness of the cause to which he is calling the nation. Black marks parade in disciplined fashion across numbered pages. In one case, these marks report what had just happened elsewhere; in another, they chronicle what occurred long ago; in a third, they create a world that has never existed nor even could. Actors appear on a stage, exchanging words and gestures, doing this and that; images appear on a screen, with one scene "following" another, though not in any straightforward chronological sequence; colors appear on a canvas; the notes of a composition are translated into sounds by the exertions of musicians.

Semiotics is nothing less than the study of footprints, fossils, symptoms, traffic signals, bodily gestures, visual messages, literary texts, dramatic performances, visual artworks, and so on insofar as each of these acts like a sign. Certain forms of signs have been, in some cases, the formal objects of inquiry for a very long time: Doctors have studied symptoms, linguists have studied words, biologists the dances of bees, rhetoricians the figures of speech, anthropologists the symbols of humankind, and theologians the stories of the gods. But, beginning in the second half of the nineteenth century, the bold dream of an inclusive theory of signs—an investigation that would bring into a single fold all species of signs and thus all modes of meaning—took hold of the American philosopher Charles Sanders Peirce (1839–1914) and, a little later, of the Swiss linguist Ferdinand de Saussure (1857–1913). "A great desideratum is," according to Peirce, "a general theory of all possible kinds of signs, their modes of signification, of denotation, and of information; and their whole behaviour and properties . . ." (MS 634; quoted by Fisch, p. 340). "A science that studies the life of signs within society is," according to Saussure, "conceivable" (p. 16). He proposed to call it *semiologie* and observed that "[s]ince the science does not yet exist, no one can say what it would be like; but it has a right to exist, a place staked out in advance."

In the eyes of its advocates today, semiotics as a distinct field of inquiry not only has firmly established its right to exist but is beginning to secure the audience it deserves— an international community of scholars drawing upon deep historical learning no less than contemporary theoretical developments. Even skeptics are obliged to concede that semiotics has influenced, often deeply, numerous disciplines, including literary theory, literary criticism, legal theory, philosophy, theology, psychology, sociology, and anthropology. Even if skeptics attempt to combat this influence and hence to fight semiotics, they can do so only by joining the debate; and they can do this only by virtue of understanding the terms of the debate. So, even though this glossary has been written by someone and for those sympathetic to the project of articulating and refining a comprehensive theory of signs, it should be useful to those who contest or even reject this project.

Put in the most cynical light, semiotics might appear as simply one of the more recent and arcane academic fads whose demise is devoutly to be wished. But a speedy demise is highly improbable and this dismissive judgment entirely unfair. Semiotics is not a fashion emanating out of Paris, doomed to be passé before too long; it is an angle of vision rooted in a long and rich history. Plato and Aristotle, Augustine and Aquinas, Ockham and Poinsot are part of this history, as are Hobbes and Locke, Leibniz and Hegel—to mention but a few.

In the course of this history, the study of signs has generated a vast, complex, truly exciting though often dishearteningly difficult literature. The purpose of this little book is to lessen the likelihood that that vast literature will be a closed book to undergraduates and others whose interests in either semiotics itself or literature, anthropology, theology, philosophy, and the like lead them to consult the writings of such theorists as Peirce or Saussure, Roman Jakobson or Susanne Langer, Louis Hjelmslev or A. J. Greimas, Roland Barthes or Julia Kristeva, Umberto Eco or Jacques Derrida. Words are, in a way, magical. When the deaf-mute child Helen Keller grasped the meaning of water—when she correlated the "letters" impressed on her hand by her teacher Anne Sullivan with the cool liquid she felt but a moment before—a world opened itself to a mind imprisoned in darkness and silence. In a less dramatic but essentially similar way, when the user of this glossary forges unfamiliar connections, makes new correlations, a world also opens up. The world of semiotics becomes thereby an open book.

A

Abduction. A term used by Charles S. **Peirce** to designate the process of **inference** by which a **hypothesis** is formed or generated; the result of such a process—the inference drawn or the guess proffered. Also called **retroduction** and hypothesis.

The word "abduction" is ambiguous (see **ambiguity**): It possesses more than one meaning, and these meanings are likely to be confused or conflated. In one sense, the term means the forceful or unlawful act of carrying off someone or something; in semiotics it concerns the discovery of a law or some other factor that would render some phenomenon intelligible. In addition, *abduction*, as it comes to semiotics from Peirce, is primarily a logical (rather than a psychological) process. While psychology is a descriptive and explanatory science, **logic** is a **normative science**.

Most of Sherlock Holmes's so-called deductions are, strictly speaking, abductions—guesses about what took place. They are guesses carefully framed and then carefully tested. In classifying abduction as an inference, Peirce is claiming that, along with **deduction** and **induc-**

tion, abduction is susceptible to logical analysis and evaluation: It can be broken down into units or parts and, in addition, can be judged in light of its function (explaining in a trustworthy way what is puzzling). Abduction differs from the two other forms of inference. Deduction is the logical operation by which we derive the necessary consequences from some purely hypothetical situation (for example, if it is true that A is greater than B and B is greater than C, then it is also necessarily true that A is greater than C). Induction is the operation by which we test hypotheses in terms of consequences derived by deduction; abduction is that by which hypotheses are framed in the first place. In other words, deduction proves that something *must* be the case; induction shows that something *actually is* the case; and abduction suggests that something *might be* the case (CP 5.171).

While treating abduction as a form of inference implies that there is for Peirce a logic of discovery, this logic should not be taken as a simple recipe for cooking up reliable guesses. There are, for example, several ways of improving one's chances in playing the game of Twenty Questions; one way is to move from the general to the specific. The logic of discovery, in Peirce's sense at least, is nothing more—but nothing less—than the various rules and procedures by which we enhance our chances of guessing right.

Abject, the. A term used by Julia **Kristeva** to designate that which upsets, disturbs, or undermines some established order or stable position. It does so because it is in between what we ordinarily take to be absolute opposites (for example, life and death, or the human and the mechanical).

A number of English words are derived from the Latin *jacere*, "to throw." Some of these words (*subject, object,*

2

and *abject*) are important for semiotics. Etymologically, the **subject** (*sub* = under) is that which is thrown under, or subjected to, some process; the **object** (*ob* = against) is that which throws itself against, or resists, another; and the abject is that which is thrown off, away, or from. The abject is neither subject nor object; rather, it is something that "disturbs identities, systems and orders. Something that does not respect limits, positions, rules. The in-between, the ambiguous, the mixed up" (Kristeva 1980, 12). A corpse is an example of the abject, for it is neither human nor nonhuman—it is in between and mixed up. A mother's body is for a child something abject, something both belonging to and not belonging to the child.

The abject is, according to Kristeva, a key factor in the formation of **subjectivity** (or the "**I**"). Early in the process of forming an identity (a process involving a transition from the pre-Oedipal **semiotic** level to the **symbolic** level), the abject contributes to the child's separation from the mother. But the formation of identity is a continuous process in which the semiotic dimension of subjectivity and language often disrupts the symbolic order. So, throughout our lives, the abject operates to disturb identity, system, and order. Since our identity and stability as subjects are derived from the unity and stability of the objects to which we attach ourselves, the abject by its very nature poses a threat to our subjectivity. The formation of subjectivity is a complex, ongoing, precarious process in which we witness, on the one hand, the blurring of the boundaries between self and other and, on the other hand, the ability of the self to distinguish itself from others. Jacques **Lacan**, Luce **Irigaray**, Kristeva and other semioticians have explored this process in depth and detail; a distinctive feature of Kristeva's *semanalytic* account of human subjectivity is her attention to the role played by the abject.

Abridgement. The reduction or shortening of a word or expression; for example, the abridgement of of "metropolitan" to "metro." Abridgment affects **signifiers** other than words (that is, ones other than **verbal** or **linguistic** signifiers). The barest hint of a nod may come to replace, in a person's repertoire of nonverbal communication, the act of nodding the head up and down several times. Here, as in the case of the shortening of verbal signifiers, we see at work the principle of economy (the principle according to which the maximum of achievement is sought via the minimum of effort). This principle is, however, only one among other principles at work in language and other sign systems. No single principle can account for the complex operation of any sign system; even so, a tendency toward economy is a feature of all sign systems.

Abstraction. The process by which certain features of a **phenomenon** or **reality** are selected for consideration, to the neglect of other features; or the product resulting from such a process. The product or result derived from this process is an *ens rationis*, a being of reason: a being encountered only in thought. If we focus on human beings simply as economic actors to the exclusion of all other dimensions, then we have produced an abstraction. Charles S. **Peirce** who distinguished between two types of abstraction, **hypostatic** and **prescissive** (see, for example, CP 4.235), pointed out that "[a]bstractions have been the butt of ridicule in modern times" (CP 4.234). We often condemn or disparage a position or form of thinking by calling it abstract. But, in themselves, the processes by which we form abstract conceptions and the resulting abstractions deserve our respect. All thought selects some highly salient feature of an object, neglecting all others.

Abstraction is nothing less than a *conditio sine qua non* for thinking at all. This is as true of practical thought as it is of highly theoretical thought. When an individual jumps out of the way of an onrushing car, that action reflects a high-level abstraction: For the purpose of maintaining life and limb, the individual takes the approaching object to be nothing but a threat. The individual selects—in this example, instantaneously—a single aspect of a complex whole and, for the purpose at hand, takes that aspect to be practically equivalent to the whole while ignoring all other aspects. The whole of the car's reality is reduced to a single feature. Such a conception is not only highly abstract, it is also preeminently practical. Precisely because it is abstract, because it selects that feature most directly—and urgently—pertinent to some purpose or desire (here, the avoidance of injury or worse). Thus, in the name of practicality no less than that of theory, abstraction should be esteemed, not demeaned.

Actant. A term introduced by A. J. **Greimas** and adopted by narratologists to designate the most basic **categories** of plot development. Originally, Greimas proposed that there are three such categories, each one a **binary opposition:** subject/object, sender/receiver, helper/opponent. (He was guided in the identification of these categories by V. I. Propp, who in *Morphology of the Folktale* analyzed folktales in terms of the villain, the donor, the helper, the princess or person sought after and her father, the dispatcher, the hero, and the false hero.) Eventually, however, Greimas relegated helper/opponent to the status of **auxiliant.** The actantial roles are often performed by a specific character in a narrative. An actantial role is, however, a **function** that is not necessarily identifiable with any specific character or person in a narrative; more than one character (the *acteur* as distinct from the actant) may perform this function. In addition, the function may be assigned to a nonhuman entity or even an inanimate object (for example, a shark may function as an opponent or the Batmobile may be the helper).

An *acteur* within a given narrative plays a role or number of roles in the overall economy of the plot development (for example, Merlin plays the role of helper in the Arthurian legend). When this is not the case, we judge the story to be flawed. Just as a poorly constructed sentence violates a grammar, so too does a poorly wrought narrative. This implies that there is a grammar of narrative. Greimas and other contemporary semioticians have devoted themselves to discovering just such a grammar. Their interest is not prescriptive but explanatory; that is, their interest is not in stating the rules that all narrators must follow but in identifying the mechanisms by which meaning, at the level of narrative, is generated.

The drive to conceive of plot development in terms of abstract functions is thus connected with the drive to uncover the grammar of narrative. Such a grammar aims at isolating the most basic units of some semiotic field and then discovering the laws by which such units are assembled. **Actantial analysis** is a technique used by narratologists and, more generally, readers to make sense out of stories.

Actantial analysis. The **analysis** of a **narrative** in terms of **actants,** the abstract functions found at the level of deep structure. For narratologists such as Roland **Barthes** and A. J. **Greimas,** narrative discourse possesses both a surface structure and a deep structure. What takes place on the surface of a narrative is ordinarily described in terms of characters (*acteurs*), actions, events, etc.; what underlies this is alleged to be a grammar, a set of rules according to which the elementary units of narrative discourse (frequently called narremes) are formed and combined. Actantial analysis is an approach to narrative discourse inspired by the success of **structuralist** approaches to such apparently diverse **phenomena** as language, culture, kinship, cuisine, and so on.

Acteme. A term proposed by Kenneth L. Pike for the most basic unit in the analysis of communicative behavior, whether the behavior is **verbal** or **nonverbal.** What the phoneme is to the study of language as a system of aural signs, the acteme is to the study of communication as a behavioral system.

While Pike's distinction between **emic** and **etic** research has been highly influential, his terms *acteme* and *behavioreme* are not used outside a rather narrow circle. These terms nonetheless provide an illustration of a pervasive and important tendency in contemporary **semiotics:** to apply the model of **structuralist linguistics** to something other than **language.** From this perspective, language is to be explained by the identification of its most basic units (**phonemes** at the level of sound and **sememes** at the level of meaning) and the discovery of its most basic combinatorial laws. Within any given language, only certain ways of combining the most basic units are permissible or legitimate. An account of the language is adequate (see **adequacy**) only to the extent that it discovers the rules governing how the most basic units can be combined and, of course, these units themselves.

Pike's terms are intended to provide the resources for analyzing and investigating any form of behavior, verbal or otherwise. Likewise, a general theory of signs is a theory of signs in general, not of this or that species of signs but of anything that might meaningfully be called a sign. The drive to attain such generality can be observed

7

in countless contexts, even those in which an investigator is preoccupied with bringing into manageable shape some specific field of semiotic inquiry.

Acteur. An "actor" or character at the surface level of a narrative discourse, in contrast to the abstract function of **actant** at the level of **deep structure.**

Actuality. A mode of **being** distinct from potentiality. Things do not merely exist in various shapes and sizes; the very way one thing *is* can vary from the way other things *are*. While a newborn is only a potential member of some linguistic community, the competent users of a given language are actual members of that community. One might (as, for example, **Aristotle** did) distinguish between grades or levels of actuality. Attaining a competency (say, acquiring the capacity to speak a language) differentiates one from those who have the potential to attain this capacity but have not yet done so. But the actual exercise of an acquired competency (the *act* of speaking) marks a fuller realization of one's actuality as a speaker. The actual acquisition of a competency is a distinct level of actuality from that of the actual exercise of that competency. The manner in which I *am* a typist, while actually typing, is different from the way in which I *am* a swimmer while not actually swimming.

Because the investigation of signs has been, from classical to contemporary times, a lively interest of philosophical inquirers, and because questions concerning the nature and modes of being have been at, or at least near, the center of philosophy, **semiotics** (the study of signs) and metaphysics (reflection on the nature and modes of being) have crisscrossed at a number of important points. This has given rise to an intricate and intriguing conceptual tapestry, distinctively metaphysical conceptions being woven together with semiotic ones to create arresting patterns and suggestive configurations.

In the writings of Charles S. **Peirce** we find just such a tapestry. There are, according to him, three modes of being (see, for example, CP 1.23). When we say that something might have been or might be, we are calling attention to things quite different from those that have been, are now, or will be; and both of these are distinct from what would be. It is possible to subsume these under three headings: "every Object is either a Can-be, an Actual, or a Would-be" (CP 8.305). My being as a novelist is that of a mere might-be or can-be (since I have never written a novel, nor do the circumstances of my life appear to be conducive to the completion of such a work); my being as a lexicographer is, especially at this moment, an actuality; and, finally, my being as a lover of jazz is a would-be (given the opportunity and leisure, I would take great delight in listening to, say, Scott Hamilton at Fat Tuesday's or Shirley Horn at the Village Vanguard). While all three modes of being are relevant to Peirce's lifelong investigation of signs, the third mode is especially pertinent. It is in fact the very mode of being exhibited by signs.

Actualization. The process by which something merely potential becomes actual (for example, the growth of a flower from a seed). A. J. **Greimas** and J. Courtes explain that, in the context of semiotics, this term designates "the passage from system to process. Thus, language [*langue*] is a virtual system which is actualized in speech [*parole*] and in discourse" (1982, 9). When a code is used to convey a message (when, for example, English as a *langue* or system is put to work to produce sentences), the code becomes actualized in and through these sentences.

9

It should not be supposed that the code or *langue* is an inert instrument in the hands of personal agents who have their being and power apart from their semiotic competencies (that is, their capacity to produce and interpret signs of various sorts). For many semioticians, these codes or systems have a life and **agency** of their own: They themselves are impersonal agents or forces, acting upon and through personal agents (or speaking subjects). See also **actuality, anti-humanism.**

Addressee. One of the six factors making up any speech event or **communication** process. The addressee is the being to whom a message is addressed or conveyed; the **addresser** is the agent or mechanism that sends or transmits a message. If I shout across the street to warn you of some danger, you are the addressee while I am the addresser.

In addition to the addressee and addresser, the other factors in any communicative process are **context, message, contact,** and **code.** Corresponding to each of these factors is a **function.** Insofar as communication is directed toward the addressee, its function is **conative**; insofar as its is directed toward the addresser, its function is **expressive.** If I say "Bella donna, meet me at the piazza this evening," the addressee is the focus of the communication and, thus, its function is conative. If I say "My heart is broken because she never came," I, in the role of addresser, am the focus; thus the function of the message is expressive.

Various synonyms for this pair of addresser/addressee are, respectively: sender/receiver; communicator/recipient; emitter/receiver; source/destination; encoder/decoder; speaker/listener-hearer; writer/author-reader. Charles **Peirce** sometimes used the terms **utterer** and **interpreter** to designate sender and receiver.

To characterize the addressee of a message as an author-reader underscores the active, indispensable role the addressee plays in the construction of meaning. The meaning of a **text** is not a fully finished product to be consumed; it is a finely woven process to be enacted and re-enacted by readers. These readers are, in the very act of reading, authoring (or, at least, co-authoring) the meaning of a text ordinarily written by someone else. Hence there arises the need to distinguish between the *author* and the *writer* of a text. See also **author, death of the.**

Addresser. One of the six factors in any communicational exchange (see **communication**); specifically, the agent or mechanism that sends or transmits a **message.** (See **addressee.**)

Corresponding to this factor is a distinctive function, namely, the **expressive** or **emotive** function. When a communicative process focuses on the agent sending the message, its function is expressive or emotive. For example, if a person says "I am tired," the function of this message often is to reveal something about the addresser. It is conceivable that, in some contexts, this same proposition might perform a **conative** rather than an expressive function. For it might mean "Let's go home," in which case the addressee, rather than the addresser, is the focus of the exchange. This example shows the importance of **context** in ascertaining the meaning of any message. It also indicates that what might seem to be a statement of fact is not that at all, or not principally that. In our example, in uttering "I am tired," the speaker is in effect making a request that the addressee do something (leave with the speaker).

Adequacy (observational, descriptive, and **explanatory).** Three virtues or strengths of a theory moving, respectively, from the minimal requirement of

11

observational adequacy to the ultimate goal of explanatory adequacy, by way of the intermediate desideratum of descriptive adequacy. This threefold distinction can be best explained by an example. Consider a theory of language. Such a theory possesses *observational* adequacy if it provides us with the means of generating or producing all and only those strings of words competent users of the language would intuitively recognize as correct or grammatical. The theory is said to possess *descriptive* adequacy (or to be descriptively adequate) if it also provides the resources for describing why within the language certain strings make sense and other strings are nonsense. The theory must provide these resources, again, in an intuitively convincing way to competent users of the language. But the ultimate goal of any linguistic inquiry aspiring to scientific status is to move beyond mere observation and description to explanation (see **Erklarung**). A theory of language possesses *explanatory* adequacy when it identifies the mechanisms or devices by which meaningful or grammatical sentences are generated.

Adequatio. Latin word meaning equivalence, equality, or correspondence. Adequation is the process whereby one thing is made equal to something else. In **medieval** thought, truth was defined in terms of *adequatio*. Truth was said by Thomas Aquinas to be an *adequatio rei et intellectus*. In other words, truth is a correspondence between what we think and what we are thinking about—in short, between our intellects and reality. If an idea is true, it is in a certain respect equal to the object it claims to represent; if it is false, there is a disproportion or lack of equivalence between thought and thing.

The so-called correspondence theory of truth has been rejected by some highly influential contemporary thinkers. One important reason given for this rejection is that this conception of truth suggests far too simple and uniform a notion. If when confronted with the question "What is truth?" we take Ludwig **Wittgenstein**'s advice to look and see how the adjective "true" and the adverb "truthfully" actually function in ordinary language, we discover that no simple formula can capture the essence of truth. Indeed, the very supposition that there *is* an essence of truth is hereby called into question. The various but equally legitimate uses of "true" and "truthfully" suggest a motley association of conceptions bound together not by a single essence (or common nature) but by a crisscrossing network of **family resemblances.** Our task thus becomes not extracting a single essence from these various **usages** but paying painstaking attention to the various ways "truth" and its cognates are used. What William James (1842–1910) called our "craving for generality" must not be allowed to blunt our attention to the particulars and our discernment of irreducible variety. When this craving is held in check, simple formulas such as truth as *adequatio* will be seen not to capture *the* essence of truth but merely to describe one legitimate but quite narrow usage of a truly protean word.

Though this critique of the correspondence theory has been highly influential, the theory still has its advocates. The question of truth continues to be a pivot around which philosophical and other forms of debate turn. Though we may never get to the bottom of the truth about truth, for philosophers and others the quest itself justifies the effort.

Adjuvant. French term meaning helper, used by A. J. **Greimas** to designate what originally was conceived as an actantial role (see **actant**) and what eventually became classified as an **auxiliant.**

13

Aesthetic function of language. The **function** linked to the aspect of **communication** known as the **message;** also called the **poetic function.** In any process of **communication,** an **addresser** conveys a **message** to an **addressee;** this process takes place in a **context** and depends on both a **code** and some form of contact or **channel** between the addresser and addressee. Connected with each constituent of communication is a function: The emotive **function** is linked to the addresser, the **conative** to the addressee, the referential to the context, the **phatic** to the contact, the **metalingual** to the code, and the aesthetic or poetic to the message itself.

Today, many assume that, in a literary text, language is being used not to express the feelings of the authors, to direct the actions of the readers, or to refer to objects or events in the world; rather, language is being used here to reveal the power and nature of language itself. This conception of the aesthetic function of language or communication (a conception found, for example, in the writings of Roman **Jakobson**) tends to be formalist rather than contextualist, for it locates this function in the inherent form of the literary (or artistic) **text.** To do this requires abstracting from the psychobiographical context of the author's life and also from the historical contexts in which the text was written and in which the text is being read. Extreme formalism is, however, an untenable position. As Virginia Woolf notes, "fiction is like a spider's web, attached ever so lightly perhaps, but still attached to life [or reality] at all four corners" (1929 [1957], 43). To appreciate fully such a web, one must both trace carefully the intricate pattern or form of the web itself *and* explore its points of attachment. *Formal* consideration of the aesthetic text as a self-contained and auto-referential system needs to be supplemented by *contextual* considerations of various sorts.

Ad hoc. Latin expression meaning "to this," used as an adjective to describe something (for example, a committee or **hypothesis**) specifically designed to address a particular problem, issue, or objective. If an administrator at a university organizes a committee having the charge of addressing itself *to this* issue (say, security on campus), that official would have established an ad hoc committee. Ordinarily such committees are of short duration; once the issue is resolved, they are disbanded. An ad hoc hypothesis is one designed to plug a hole in a theory. For example, when the geocentric (earth-centered) view of Ptolemy and other astronomers was shown to conflict with the improved observations of the heavenly bodies, proponents of this view devised the ad hoc hypothesis of epicycles: The planets do not merely circle the earth but they move in small circles (epicycles) along the line of their circular orbit. Eventually it became necessary, in order to square the Ptolemaic view with the observational data, to suppose that the planets moved in an incredibly complex pattern of epicycles. In general, the need to devise ad hoc hypotheses to maintain a theory is taken as symptomatic of a deficiency in the theory, though it is not necessarily a compelling reason to reject the theory outright.

Ad hominem. Latin expression meaning "to the person," ordinarily used as an **abridgment** of *argumentum ad hominem*. In one sense, this means an **argument** addressed specifically to a person (for example, "If you hold this or assume that, you cannot consistently maintain this other position") and thus one usually limited in its logical force. In a quite different sense, it means a fallacious or invalid

15

form of refutation that attacks the person putting forth an argument rather than addressing the reasons put forth by that person in support of some **conclusion:** "He's a liberal so we know his proposal will involve needless spending and yield—at best—minimal results." The castigation of individuals and, by implication, of their positions by hurling epithets (in this case, the L-word—liberal) is the most common form of this fallacious move. Though logically flawed, ad hominem refutations are often rhetorically forceful: They persuade people, on irrelevant grounds, to reject the conclusion of an argument.

Aesthetics. In a broad sense, the branch of philosophy dealing with beauty as it is encountered in both art and nature. As it is ordinarily used today, however, this definition of aesthetics is, in one sense, too broad and, in another, too narrow. It is too broad because the scope of aesthetics is today usually limited to human artifacts. Natural phenomena such as seascapes and sunsets obviously fall outside this scope. But the definition is also too narrow, for contemporary practitioners do not devote themselves primarily, if at all, to exploring the nature and forms of beauty. While classical aesthetics strove to define beauty in general (take, for example, the definition of the beautiful found in Thomas Aquinas's writings as that which pleases or delights upon being perceived) and to develop the criteria by which beautiful objects could be identified, the principal concern of contemporary aesthetics is with the nature of art itself and, even more generally, with processes of signification. We rarely ask of artworks "Is it beautiful?," but we frequently wonder "Is this art?" or "What does it mean?" Much contemporary art is a self-conscious experimentation with various and often mixed media for the purpose of exposing sham meanings and of establishing unusual resonances. According to one highly influential approach, **Russian formalism,** the function of art is to make the familiar strange. Such art is a field that invites investigation from a semiotic viewpoint.

Agency. Having the status or capacity of an agent—a person, mechanism, or any other thing by which some process is initiated and perhaps sustained, or by which some force is exerted and some change is produced. We tend to think of agents as persons, but an important emphasis of contemporary semiotics is that systems of signs are themselves inherently vital and powerful forces, capable of shaping the way human beings and other users of signs think and feel as well as speak and write. Thus sign systems themselves may be considered agents.

Agreeableness to reason, method of. One of four methods of **inquiry,** or ways of fixing **beliefs,** distinguished by Charles S. **Peirce**; also called the **a priori** method. According to advocates of this method, we should adopt in our struggle to overcome doubt that belief which is most agreeable to our individual reason. "Agreeable to reason" does not mean what agrees with experience, but what we find ourselves disposed to believe. Like the methods of tenacity and of **authority,** this method is fatally flawed, its fatal flaw being that it "makes of inquiry something similar to the development of taste; but taste, unfortunately, is always more or less a matter of fashion . . ." (CP 5.383). Unlike the method of **science,** these three ways of fixing belief do not take **experience** seriously enough; nor do they conceive **reality** adequately. In our saner moments, we realize that reality is not simply what we are inclined to suppose; it is what it is quite apart from our conceptions of it. The only truly responsible way of fixing our beliefs is one uncompromisingly committed to such a notion of reality—and humbly open to the ways

17

reality reveals itself in and through our experience. So, at least, argues Peirce.

Algorithm. In mathematics, a procedure for solving a problem that takes a finite number of steps and often involves repeating an operation; more generally, a step-by-step procedure for attaining some goal or resolving some difficulty.

Alienation effect or **A-effect.** The usual translation of the German expressions *Verfremdungseffekt* or *V-effekt*, terms used by Bertolt Brecht (1898–1956) to designate the intentional effect of dispelling the realistic illusion of a dramatic performance. Audiences need to be jarred into the realization that what they are seeing is *not* real, for only then do they cease to be passively receptive and can then become critically engaged in the process. One device by which this effect might be accomplished is to have an actor step out of character and comment on how poorly another actor is performing. See also **defamiliarization.**

Aliquid stat pro aliquo. Latin expression meaning "something stands for something else." The function of one thing standing for another (**stare pro**) has, from ancient to contemporary times, been taken as *the* essential characteristic of signs. One influential formulation of this view is found in Augustine's *De doctrina christiana*: "A sign is a thing which, over and above the impressions it makes on the senses, causes something else to come into the mind as a consequence of itself." One might hear the sound Florence or Firenze and think of a city, or see smoke and think of fire. The power of the sound to convey a conception of the city and the power of a sight to suggest the cause of its appearance illustrates what the formula *aliquid stat pro aliquo* means, for the interpreter of these signs takes something to stand for something else.

But the status or nature of the *aliquo* (that for which the sign stands) has been, from ancient times, a matter of controversy. In our own time, this controversy has intensified. On the one hand, there are those who contend that language and, more generally, signs of various sorts provide us with access to an extralinguistic and extrasemiotic world (a world that exists independently of language and all other systems of signs). Hence language and signs reveal what is there. On the other hand, there are those who argue that since our only access to reality is via signs of one sort or another, what we call reality amounts to nothing more than an interpretation. Specifically, it is the sum total of our most accredited and reliable interpretations. "There are," in the words of Friedrich Nietzsche (1844–1900), "no facts, only interpretations." The status and nature of what signs stand for are themselves thus open to conflicting interpretations; so much so that the function of "standing for" has been explicitly challenged. From this viewpoint, the function of signs is to generate other signs, and the function of *these* signs is to generate yet other signs, ad infinitum.

The image of signs generating other signs, rather than signs standing for extrasemiotic entities, has exerted a profound influence on contemporary thought. Semiotic systems, such as language or a body of literature, are not transparent windows through which we look at reality; they are labyrinths, perhaps even labyrinths leading into other labyrinths, from which there is no escape. According to its critics (for instance, Frederic Jameson), this view makes of language and other sign systems a prisonhouse allowing no access to the "*real* world." For its advocates, the demand to subordinate the play of signs (or signifiers) to what is not itself a sign is rooted in a tyrannical impulse to stop what can never be truly arrested—the dynamic and self-sustained generation of signs. There may very well be a healthy impulse underlying each of these rival positions—there is, on the one hand, the impulse to use language simply and plainly so that such things as hunger, violence, injustice, cruelty, and the like do not evaporate into a miasma of signs and, on the other, the impulse to use language as imaginatively as possible so that its possibilities and power reveal themselves in ever new and startling ways.

In sum, the function of a sign is, in the classical conception, representative and, in more recent approaches, productive: For the former, a sign has its *raison d'être* in representing something extrasemiotic (something not itself a sign), while for the latter, signs are mechanisms for producing other signs, ad infinitum. See also **adequatio.**

Alterity. From Latin *alter*, other. **Otherness;** diversity, difference; having the status or force of being other than and unassimilable to some system of representation. Ordinarily alterity means that which is other than some dominant viewpoint and thus that which has been (and very likely still is) devalued, discounted, and marginalized. Marginality and unassimilability are definitive of alterity. What today is designated by the terms "alterity" and "otherness" is, in some respects, close to what Peirce called "**secondness.**"

The highly abstract category of alterity or otherness is often intended to have a practical and even political focus. It is frequently used to call attention to what has been excluded from or marginalized in the dominant discourses of Western culture. Western humanism is based on the supposed sameness of all human beings; but, in practice, it has not served all humans equally well. Those who are *other than* (or different from) the dominant images of the dominant discourses are discounted, discredited, degraded, or worse. As a way of challenging this exclusion and marginalization, the rhetoric of alterity and otherness has been crafted: There is experience other than that of males, or that of heterosexuals, or whites, or Europeans. These "others" deserve a hearing; their experience is not necessarily, or even likely, the same as those who have been historically dominant. Today the emphasis has shifted from universality (what is supposedly true of all "men") to specificity (what generally fits the experience of some specific group), from sameness, homogeneity, and oneness to otherness, alterity, and plurality.

Althusser, Louis (b. 1918). A contemporary French thinker who offered a structuralist interpretation of the Marxist perspective. His treatment of **ideology** is perhaps his most important contribution to **semiotics.** His works include *For Marx* (1977), *Essays in Self-Criticism* (1978), and *Reading Capital* (1979).

Ambiguity. The property of being open to a variety of interpretations, some of which might even be contradictory; whenever any word or expression possesses several meanings and these can be easily confused.

Ampliative/explicative. *Ampliative,* an adjective used by Charles S. **Peirce** to identify those forms of reasoning which aim at increasing our knowledge (adding something truly new to the stock of what we know). In contrast, *explicative* reasoning involves explicating— making explicit and manifest what is implicit and hidden in— some truth supposed to be securely established.

Anagram. A word or phrase derived by inverting or transposing the letters of another word or phrase. An interesting and mischievous example is the derivation of "Evil's agent" by transposing the letters in "Evangelists."

Ferdinand de **Saussure** studied anagrams in Latin poetry on the supposition that "the Latin poets deliberately concealed the anagrams of proper names in their verses. He believed he had discovered a supplementary sign system, a special set of conventions for the production of meaning, and he filled many notebooks with remarks on the various types of repetitions and anagrams he had discovered" (Culler 1986, 123).

The supposition that the anagrams Saussure detected were deliberately devised is questionable. What he might have discovered is an unconscious mechanism at work in the poetic fashioning of language and presumably also in the less finely controlled usage of words as well. The repetition of sounds or letters, albeit in transposed form, might be an important factor in the production of **verbal** messages, even if the producers of such messages are unconscious of either the presence or the importance of this mechanism. Such is the way Julia **Kristeva** interprets these repetitions and transpositions. Their unconscious operation would be only another case of human agents not knowing fully what they are doing.

Analepsis. A narrative technique commonly called flashback and less often retrospection. If in the course of a **narrative** events preceding those narrated up to this point are presented, we have an instance of analepsis; if in the course of a narrative events coming after those narrated thus far are presented, we have a prolepsis or flash forward.

Analogy. In general, a comparison; a similarity between things that are otherwise different (for example, in several famous passages from his *Course on General Linguistics*, Ferdinand de **Saussure** calls attention to an analogy between language and a game of chess). In logic, a specific type of comparison having four terms and the following form or structure: A:B::C:D (A is to B as C is to D; for instance, the trunk is to an elephant what hands are to humans). Analogy is a type of inference in which the agreement of several things in some respects is used as a warrant for supposing that these things are alike in other respects.

Analysis. The process by which a phenomenon or object being investigated is broken down, either physically (as in the chemical analysis of a substance) or conceptually, into its components in order to understand more fully the phenomenon or object. Analysis is one of the most basic procedures used in any sphere of inquiry. It is, thus, on a par with observation, classification, generalization, validation, and all the other procedures undertaken, in one form or another, by human inquirers, regardless of subject matter.

Ferdinand de **Saussure** analyzed the sign into an **aural** image (the sound heard when a word or sentence is uttered) and a mental image (the concept conveyed by the utterance upon being heard); he then generalized these components into the **signifier** and the **signified.** In contrast, Charles S. **Peirce** broke semiosis or sign action into three components—the **sign** or **sign vehicle** itself, the **object,** and the **interpretant.**

Analytic/synthetic judgments. The highly influential way in which Immanuel Kant drew the distinction between "truths of reason" and "truths of fact" (a distinction found clearly drawn by, for example, David Hume and Gottfried Leibniz). One of the most common and important forms of judgment is that of predicating (from the Latin *predicare,* to say of) a quality or attribute of a subject. If I judge that "The stove is black," I predicate a quality (blackness) of a subject. Both analytic and synthetic judgments are of the subject-predicate form; the difference between them concerns how the predicate is in each case related to the subject. An analytic judgment is one in which the predicate is (to use Kant's own expression) "contained in," or entailed by, the subject. For example, the judgment that "A triangle is three-sided" is analytic since three-sidedness is contained in (or entailed by) triangularity. The judgment "The stove is black" is in contrast synthetic, since there is nothing in the concept of the subject that entails it being black. While a four-sided triangle is inconceivable, a white stove is not. The three-sidedness of triangles is a truth of reason: It is discoverable by reason without any recourse to, or reliance on, experience. The blackness of this stove is a truth of fact; only experience can teach us that this quality is attributable to this subject.

In his influential essay "Two Dogmas of Empiricism," Willard van Orman Quine called into question the possibility of drawing an absolutely sharp distinction between analytic and synthetic truths.

Animal Symbolicum. Latin expression meaning the symbolic or symbol-using animal; an expression Ernst **Cassirer** used to designate the human species. *Animal symbolicum* is intended to suggest something both wider and deeper than what is conveyed by the classical definition of the human being as a rational animal. See also *Homo loquens.*

Anthropomorphism. From the Greek words *anthropos* and *morphe,* meaning human and form. The tendency to conceive or interpret what is not human or personal in human or personal terms. To conceive of God the Father as a man with white hair and a white flowing beard is to conceive of Him anthropomorphically. So too, if I attribute maliciousness to the rock that strikes me on the head, I am in effect conceiving this inanimate thing in personal terms, specifically in terms of a will. But only voluntary agents (beings with wills of their own) can bear another malice or ill will, so this conception is misguided. In general, to show that a conception is anthropomorphic is assumed to be equivalent to showing that it is mistaken. For such conceptions seem to involve "reading into" phenomena properties or capacities that are not truly there.

Charles S. **Peirce,** however, argued against the wholesale condemnation of anthropomorphic conceptions. He claimed that humans are so completely hemmed in by the bounds of their possible practical experience, their minds are so consistently employed as an instrument of their needs and desires, that they cannot in the least mean anything that transcends the limits of such experience. From this he concluded: " 'Anthropomorphic' is what pretty much all [human] conceptions are at bottom" (CP 5.47).

Anthroposemiosis. All of the sign processes in which human beings participate but which other animals may also use; more narrowly, the distinctively *human* uses and forms of signs. Art, science, religion, and language itself are all, at least in their more complex and sophisticated manifestations, examples of anthroposemiosis in the more limited sense. Whatever is unique or characteristic of a particular species of animal is said to be species-specific. Anthroposemiosis might refer to either the entire range of human semiosis (including those exhibited by other species of animal) or, more narrowly, only those forms of semiosis that are species-specific to *homo sapiens.*

Anthroposemiotics. That branch of **semiotics** devoted to investigating the human, especially the distinctively or uniquely human, uses and forms of signs; that part of **zoosemiotics** concerned with **anthroposemiosis.**

Anti-humanism. Opposition to, or rejection of, **humanism.** In a very broad sense, humanism is simply the affirmation of the value and dignity of human beings; in a more restricted sense, it refers to a cultural and intellectual movement, beginning in the Renaissance (if not even earlier) and animated by a specific image of human beings. **Consciousness, autonomy** (understood principally in the negative sense of freedom from the constraints of tradition and the will of tyrants), individuality, and control over nature are among the most salient features of this image. This vision of humanity has been opposed for a number of reasons, not the least of which is that while it pretends to be a universally valid portrait serving all human beings equally well (regardless of class, gender, ethnicity, etc.), it is a seriously distorted and ideologically biased position. Anti-humanism is, of course, the rejection (for whatever reason) of this vision of humanity. One encounters it in, for example, Michel Foucault's *The Order of Things (Les Mots et les Choses)*. If we see through the illusory nature of the humanistic conceptions of consciousness, freedom, individuality, mastery, etc., we are destined to witness the "death of man," of man as *he* has been defined and defended especially in the postmedieval epoch of Western culture. The death of God announced by Friedrich Nietzsche has turned out to be a prelude to the death of man. Such, at least, is the anti-humanistic conclusion of Foucault's *The Order of Things* (1966 [1973], esp. 384ff).

Antinomy. In general, a contradiction between what appear to be two equally valid principles or between two (apparently) correctly drawn conclusions from such principles.

Antipsychologism. The view that psychological or mental processes cannot explain **sign** processes. For advocates of this doctrine, signs are not to be explained by reference to minds, especially minds conceived as inner or private spheres; rather minds are explicable only in terms of **semiosis** or sign action. This abrupt change in one's heuristic orientation is called a **paradigm shift** by Thomas Kuhn. Hence **semiotics** (the study of signs) involves nothing less than such a shift in the way signs are understood and investigated.

In a paradigm shift, the community of inquirers or, at least, a significant segment of it not only turns from one set of concerns and questions to another; it also revises its understanding of what counts as an explanation. In the study of signs, there has been in the last hundred years a shift from psychologistic explanations of signs to semiotic explanations of mind. For some semioticians, this conceptual and **heuristic** revolution is as great and important as the one inaugurated by Galileo and carried through by Newton. In Aristotle's physics, the fact of motion, of bodies moving at all, required explanation. Galileo and, later, Newton shifted the focus of physics by assuming the motion of bodies; what needed to be explained were changes in direction and velocity.

Charles S. **Peirce** was, in his **semeiotic,** explicitly antipsychologistic. In contrast, Ferdinand de **Saussure** often characterized the sign as a psychological entity; he also classified *semiologie* itself as a branch of social psychology. From the perspective of his successors, however, Saussure provided the resources for developing an antipsychologistic theory of signs.

27

Anti-realism. The thoroughgoing rejection of realism; even more radically, the rejection of the *problématique* (or set of concerns) giving rise to the question of whether or not our signs can depict or represent reality accurately.

Aperçu. A French word meaning glimpse, insight, outline, and summary. Sometimes this word is used to designate the summary or outline of an **argument** or **narrative.**

Aphasia. Loss or impairment of the capacity to use or understand words, often resulting from brain damage. Roman **Jakobson** and other linguists have studied aphasia with the hope that such investigation would throw light on both our capacity for speech (**parole**) and the nature of **language** (*langue*).

Apodictic. Having the character of necessary truth or absolute certainty. Much of Western philosophy has involved the quest for apodictic certitude. Especially beginning in the second half of the nineteenth century, this quest has been called into question. The best that human inquirers might ever attain is probable truth, less-than-apodictic certainty. Our finitude and fallibility seem to put forever beyond our reach the sort of truth or certitude aimed at by such figures as **Plato, Aristotle, Descartes,** and **Hegel.** The admission of this does not mean an espousal of **skepticism;** it rather means the adoption of **fallibilism.**

Aporia. A Greek word meaning helplessness or difficulty in dealing with, or finding out, something. In philosophy, this term is often used to designate a conceptual or theoretical impasse to which one is brought by following out the implications of one's beliefs or convictions. Many of **Plato**'s dialogues end with a character being rendered helpless under the pressure of Socrates's cross-

28

examination. At the end of these dialogues, a character confesses, or refuses to acknowledge, that he truly does not know what he is accustomed to saying or thinking. For Socrates, the confession of ignorance is the beginning of wisdom. So too for Charles S. **Peirce,** according to whom "it is only a deep sense that one is miserably ignorant that can spur one on in the toilsome path of learning" (CP 5.583). This sense of being miserably ignorant comes from *aporias,* from those theoretical impasses to which our most cherished convictions often seem to lead. See also **antinomy.**

A posteriori. Knowledge that is derived from and, thus, dependent upon experience. **A priori** designates knowledge that is prior to, and independent of, experience. These two terms are commonly used in **epistemological** discussions.

A priori. That which is prior to, or independent of, experience. In contrast, **a posteriori** refers to that which is dependent upon experience. The question of whether there are a priori or innate ideas, ones with which we are born rather than derive from the course of experience, has been contested from ancient to contemporary times. For empiricists, the human mind is at birth a *tabula rasa* (blank slate); for rationalists, we bring ideas *to* experience as well as derive them from it. The debate between empiricists and rationalists was at the center of Western philosophy during the modern epoch or period. In our own day, the linguist Noam Chomsky (b. 1928) has argued strenuously that our acquisition of language provides clear evidence of our possessing an a priori or innate set of ideas.

A priori method. See **agreeableness to reason, method of.**

Arbitrariness. The absence of a rational justification or of an intrinsic (or natural) basis. Arbitrariness has been seen as an, if not *the*, essential feature of the **sign.** According to Ferdinand de **Saussure** and his followers, a sign is an *arbitrary* correlation between a **signifier** and a **signified.** For example, there is no intrinsic connection between the signifier D-O-G and the four-legged, furry animal signified by these letters; there is only an arbitrary (or **unmotivated**) link.

The two dominant traditions in contemporary **semiotics** differ sharply regarding how much importance should be attached to the arbitrariness of signs. For the research tradition rooted in Saussure's **semiology,** arbitrariness is crucial; for that rooted in Charles S. **Peirce**'s **semeiotic,** it is not. For Saussure, the sign is an *arbitrary* correlation of a signifier with a signified. This is a definition of sign *in general*, but it is one based on taking linguistic signs as the paradigm or model of all other signs.

The arbitrary nature of these correlations needs to be seen in light of the *social* nature of language itself. As Saussure is quick to point out, "arbitrary" should not be taken to imply that the actual choice of the signifier is left to the individual speaker. Any actual language is a determinate set of arbitrary correlations over which individual speakers have little or no control. What linguistic and other signifiers mean is what the linguistic or semiotic system dictates. Here we see a distinctive emphasis of structuralist thought (structuralism having its roots in Saussure's linguistics): System as a set of constraint is stressed, the self as a source of innovation is downplayed and, in extreme cases, denied.

Throughout the history of thought, issues concerning the relationship between nature and **convention** have occupied center stage. In the ancient and medieval periods of Western culture, nature tended to be privileged and convention disparaged (as the very expression *"merely* conventional" suggests). Today the balance has shifted dramatically. For example, most appeals to human nature are immediately challenged, if not curtly dismissed; for what is called "human nature" is seen by many to be only a social construction (in other words, a historically evolved and evolving set of conventions). The Saussurean and structuralist emphasis on the arbitrariness of the sign is an example of this dramatic shift in emphasis from the naturally (and often divinely) ordained to the conventionally established. Formerly it was often supposed that what nature and God have wrought cannot, or should not, be unmade; today it is characteristically assumed that what human beings have devised in their historical struggles to gain dominance over nature and one another can, and should, be questioned, if not remade.

If language is essentially a set of arbitrary correlations, and if furthermore it is (as Saussure thought) heuristically *the* model by which all other sign systems should be understood, then it might provide a means of exposing "mythologies" and "ideologies" for what they are—human constructions wrought and maintained in the interest of certain groups and, inevitably, to the disadvantage of other groups. Thus (to cite a famous example), when Roland Barthes comments on the cover photograph of *Paris-Match* in which a black African in a French uniform is saluting a French flag, the photograph as signifier not only denotes this figure in this pose but also connotes that "France is a great colonial Empire with loyal black citizens in its army, etc." During France's conflict with Algeria, such a message obviously serves the cause of continuing colonialism. By denoting something actual (black Africans loyal to French imperialism), the photo is promoting something ideological and, in a sense, mythological. As Barthes notes, "myth does not deny things . . . [but]

31

purifies them": It "makes them innocent, it gives them a *natural* and eternal justification" (emphasis added).

Semiotics, construed not as a theoretical investigation of semiotic phenomena but as a cultural **critique** of our actual semiotic practices, often aims to see through this supposed innocence, to render problematic the "natural and eternal justification" of what are at least arguably unjust and exploitative practices (for example, the images of sexy, submissive women which so abound in our culture).

Arche-. Prefix derived from a Greek word meaning both source and ruler. Thus it conveys the sense of both that from which something comes and that by which something is ruled, regulated, or governed. Much of postmodern thought is devoted to challenging the legitimacy of searching for either an absolute origin of signs or a complete mastery of meaning. It is, in short, anarchical.

Archetypes. In general, an original type or exemplar upon which other things are modeled; in Jungian psychology, a predisposition or idea (such as the figure of the sage) rooted in the collective unconscious and open to myriad manifestations (from Merlin in the Arthurian legend to Yoda in Star Wars).

Due largely to the influence of Sigmund Freud, we are accustomed to distinguishing between the conscious and the unconscious regions of the human mind. In conceiving the relationship between the two, we sometimes rely on a spatial **metaphor** in which **consciousness** is represented as a relatively superficial region and the unconscious as a deep, dark, underlying region from which forces can explode upward, occasionally reaching the surface (that is, entering consciousness, in however disguised a form). But the unconscious so conceived is ordinarily supposed to be the product of our individual experiences,

32

especially traumatic ones occurring at a rather early age. Carl Jung maintained that, in addition to an individual unconscious, there is a **collective unconscious,** a region of the human psyche inscribed with "ideas" not resulting from our individual experience but part of our racial inheritance: The archetypes are rooted in the experience of the human race, not that of any individual human. Just as a principal objective of Freudian psychoanalysis is to put us in contact with certain crucial factors within our individual unconscious, thereby freeing us from their debilitating effect, so a primary goal of Jungian psychology is to put us in touch with our collective unconscious.

Jung's notion of archetype and, indeed, other parts of his thought reveal a deep and penetrating appreciation of the role symbols play in our individual and collective lives. If for no other reason, his work is important to **semiotics.**

Arche-writing. A term used by Jacques **Derrida** to designate the process by which signs are generated. Signs are, according to him, the **traces** or inscriptions left by the play of differences, arche-writing being nothing other than this play of differences.

Traditionally it has been assumed that spoken language is primary and written language derivative. But, according to Derrida in *Of Grammatology* and other writings, this assumed hierarchy contributes to the metaphysics of **presence** (the attempt to define Being in terms of some form of presence) and, thus, it needs to be challenged. Central to this challenge is Derrida's questioning of the hierarchy implied in conceiving speech as primary and writing as derivative.

Signs are not lifeless entities awaiting some consciousness, human or divine, to breathe life into them. They exhibit a life of their own. See **agency.** Inherent in them is a vitality, a power to grow and to replicate themselves. If we take writing in a very broad sense to mean traces of signs whose inherent dynamic propels us beyond themselves, then writing has to be taken as the *arche* or source. Derrida is, in some respects, a dialectical thinker in the tradition of Hegel; he delights in ironic reversals. In *The Phenomenology of Spirit,* Hegel shows how masters depend upon and, in a way, are enslaved to their own slaves; in *Of Grammatology* Derrida tries to show how the supposedly derivative form of language (writing) is actually primary. See also **trace, writing.**

Architectonic. A term used by Immanuel Kant and adopted by Charles S. **Peirce** to describe the systematic rather than haphazard manner in which inquiry ought to be conducted. It might be suggested that we do not know enough to construct a system of knowledge. But this suggestion might be countered by the claim that, precisely because we do not know enough, we need a system—or, at least, we need to proceed systematically.

In his *Critique of Pure Reason,* Kant offered this definition: "By an architectonic I understand the art of constructing systems" (p. 653). Since scientific knowledge is marked first and foremost by its *systematic* form, the "architectonic is the doctrine of the scientific in our knowledge." See also **scientificity.**

Architecture. The art of building explored as a means not of providing shelter but of conveying meaning. Very rarely do distinctively human activities or artifacts serve one purpose or perform one function; they are characteristically **polyfunctional.** Clothes, cars, houses, and cities each in their own way illustrate this point. In wearing these clothes or driving this car, a person is often—perhaps always—making a statement, though not necessarily a conscious one. In addition, our built environment, ranging from the small corners over which we exercise minute control (the rooms in our houses) to the vast stretches that take shape due to the confluence of countless forces (neighborhoods and cities), truly express our lives and in turn express themselves in and through our lives. The semiotics of architecture explores the specific ways the built environment provides means for expression and, in addition, the ways this environment itself is an expressive force, structuring the way we move, see and even feel. This exploration is closely related to **aesthetics, proxemics** (the semiotics of space), **zoosemiotics,** and no doubt other disciplines (some explicitly semiotic in outlook and others not). This exploration is undertaken in earnest, as Roland **Barthes** notes, when we move from metaphorical discussions of the "language of the city" to analytic and systematic research devoted to identifying architectural signs and codes.

Ferdinand de **Saussure** in his *Cours de linguistique generale* and later Ludwig **Wittgenstein** in his *Philosophical Investigations* compare language to a city. In the semiotics of architecture, the comparison is reversed—the city as a configuration of buildings and other artifacts is conceived as a language.

Argument. A set of statements in which one or more premises are put forth as evidence for, or in support of, another statement (the **conclusion**); any process of thought tending to produce a belief.

In Charles S. **Peirce**'s theory of **signs,** argument is identified as a specific kind of sign. It is part of a triad or **trichotomy: rheme, dicent, argument.** This trichotomy corresponds roughly to the more traditional distinction of concept, proposition, argument.)

Argumentation. A term used by Charles S. **Peirce** to designate a formally or explicitly stated **argument.** "An

'Argument' is any process of thought tending to produce a definite belief. An 'Argumentation' is an Argument proceeding upon definitely formulated premisses" (CP 6.456). In short, an argumentation is a formally stated argument.

Aristotle (384–322 B.C.). In his *Peri hermeneias*, translated into Latin as *De interpretatione*, this ancient Greek philosopher and scientist stated that "spoken **signs** are **symbols** of affections in the soul, and written marks [are] symbols of spoken sounds. And just as written marks are not the same for all men, neither are spoken sounds. But what these are in the first place signs of—affections of the soul—are the same for all; and what these affections are likenesses of—actual things—are also the same" (Quoted in Noth 1990, 90b). His enormous influence on later medieval thought, first Arabic and later European, alone ensures him of a significant place in the history of semiotics, for this epoch was a time when, in the context of **logic,** signs were studied with great rigor and in fine detail. Charles S. **Peirce,** who called Aristotle the greatest human intellect, also advised others to open the "dusty folios" of the medieval logicians.

Articulation. From the Latin *articulus*, meaning joint or division. In the most general sense, any process of dividing or segmenting; in linguistics, articulation ordinarily means double articulation, a feature often claimed to be unique to human speech.

Ferdinand de **Saussure** observes that "applied to speech [*parole*], articulation designates either the subdivision of a spoken chain into syllables or the subdivision of the chain of meanings into significant units" (10). At the first level of articulation, an utterance or message is divided into meaningful units (often called **sememes** and termed monemes by André Martinet—the linguist ordinarily credited

36

for formulating the principle of double articulation); at the second level, it is divided into distinguishable but meaningless sounds (**phonemes**). In written language, graphemes are the units corresponding to the phonemes of the spoken language.

The link between **language** and articulation has, from ancient times, generated a doubt regarding our ability to talk about **reality** without distorting or disfiguring it. At the level of meaning, articulation involves dividing or segmenting reality into various classes or kinds. But early in the history of both Eastern and Western thought there arose the question of whether the cuts we make—the classes we recognize or construct—truly correspond to the way the world is. Sometimes it is argued that reality is, in itself, continuous or undivided and, thus, any articulation or segmentation of it is, in principle, a distortion and perhaps even an act of violence. At other times, it has been simply thought that there is no way of determining whether our division of the world correspond to the way the world is actually structured or segmented.

Are classificatory schemes only useful fictions? Or do they have a basis in reality? Skeptics and nominalists contend that our classifications reflect our purposes and perspective, not reality's contours and character. In contrast, realists maintain that some of our classifications of reality are useful precisely because they divide reality the way it is actually divided. A map that did not in any way correspond to the terrain it purports to depict could not, in principle, fulfill the function of a map. Not all fabrications are fictions: Some of the theories and taxonomies we fabricate are more or less reliable maps for getting around in the world. This seems to entail that they correspond in some measure to the world. Such, at least, is the central claim of Peircean and other forms of **realism.**

Assertion. The act of putting forth a **proposition** as though it were true; that is, as though it merited assent or **belief.** To assert a proposition entails accepting responsibility if it turns out to be false. Charles S. **Peirce** went so far as to suggest that an assertion "is an exhibition of the fact that one subjects oneself to the penalties visited on a liar if the proposition asserted is not true" (SS 1977, 34).

Assertory. A term used by Charles S. **Peirce** to designate the fact of a sign having the property or status of an **assertion.**

According to Peirce "ordinary words in the bulk of languages are assertory. They assert as soon as they are in any way attached to any object. If you write 'Glass' upon a case, you will be understood to mean that the case contains glass" (CP 4.56).

Associative. A synonym for what today is more commonly called **paradigmatic.** *Associative* and *paradigmatic* are terms used to designate one way words or terms are related to one another in discourse; **syntagmatic** is a term used to identify a contrasting relationship among such terms (see **axis**). The meaning of an utterance is a function of *both* associative (or paradigmatic) and syntagmatic relations. In an utterance, terms are strung together. These terms are syntagmatically related to one another. But, in stringing these terms together in this way, choices were made: Certain other terms were not selected, though they might reasonably or intelligibly have been. These alternative terms are associatively or paradigmatically related to the terms actually used in the utterance. The terms actually used have, as it were, a penumbra of associations that contribute to the meaning of the utterance.

Association is the term Saussure used in contrast to syntagmatic. Because of the drive to rid linguistics of psychological terms, which Saussure frequently used (see **mentalism**), *association* was replaced by *paradigmatic*.

Aufhebung. German word meaning the reconciliation of opposites; a moment or phase of mediation; the culmination of a dialectical process. See **dialectic**.

Aufklarung. German word for **Enlightenment**.

Aural. Related to the ear or the sense of hearing. Spoken words are aural **signifiers:** They function as signifiers by virtue of being heard or being audible. In contrast, the words on this page are visual signifiers—they function as signifiers by virtue of being seen or being visible. Braille is a system of tactile signifiers—the differences that make a difference between, say, A and B are discernible by means of touch.

Austin, John Langshaw (1911–1960). An influential philosopher who taught at Oxford from 1952 to 1960. His major works are *Philosophical Papers* (1961), *Sense and Sensibilia* (1962), and *How to Do Things with Words* (1962). His account of the **locutionary, illocutionary,** and **perlocutionary force** of utterances helps the student of signs see more clearly some important features of our linguistic practice (that is, the way we use language). More generally, his work contributed to what has been called the **linguistic turn** in Anglo-American philosophy. While Austin is rightfully grouped among ordinary-language philosophers (philosophers who maintained that traditional philosophical problems are best resolved and, in many cases, "dissolved" by painstaking attention to our ordinary ways of speaking), he himself thought that this concern with language is ultimately subordinate to something else: "When we examine what we should say when, what words we should use in what situations, we are looking again not merely at words (or 'meaning,' whatever that may be) but also at the realities we use the words to talk about: We are using a sharpened awareness of words to sharpen our perceptions of, though not as the final arbiter of, the phenomena" (1961, 182). So, when addressing philosophical problems, we should realize that "ordinary language is *not* the last word [not the ultimate arbiter]: in principle it can everywhere be supplemented and improved upon and superseded. Only remember, it is the *first* word" (1961, 185).

Author, death of the. A phrase indicating a profound reorientation on the part of literary critics and theorists toward **texts.** It points to a shift in critical and theoretical attention from authors to texts and the mechanism by which texts are produced or generated.

In much contemporary literary theory and criticism, emphasis has shifted away from viewing texts as expressions of an author's ideas, attitudes, values, etc., to viewing texts as sites in which readers, by virtue of their acts of interpretation, engage in a contest to wrest meaning from signs. This recent emphasis on the reader's role in endowing the signs of the text with meaning is sometimes pushed to the point of denying any authority or importance to the author or writer (the actual producer of a text). In reading a text, we are not exploring the psyche of the author. The text is, as the word itself suggests, something woven (from the Latin *texere,* to weave); but the often intricate and always unfinished pattern woven out of signs is truly the work of the reader, not the author. Indeed, Roland **Barthes** concludes a famous essay entitled "The Death of the Author" by claiming that "the birth of the reader must be at the cost of the death of the Author" (1977, 148; cf. Foucault).

Controversies arise in literary theory and criticism over

how to recognize the rights of writers and of writings vis-à-vis the rights of author-readers. On the one hand, it seems mistaken to define the meaning of a text in terms of what has been called "authorial intent" (what is better designated here as *writer's* intent). This definition both exaggerates the authority of the historical agent (the flesh-and-blood person) who wrote the actual words out of which a text is woven *and* minimizes the autonomy writings truly have. On the other hand, it also seems mistaken to deny that there are limits to interpretation and, further, to deny the relevance of a writer's life or explicit intentions to an understanding of a literary writing. One might read Virginia Woolf's writings in light of her being the victim of sexual abuse without reducing these writings to a psychobiographical code. So, too, one might read Henry James's novels in light of his own explicit pronouncements about this genre without reducing these novels to mere illustrations of the writer's literary theory. There's more in literature than is dreamt of by writers; but their dreams and lives and objectives are an invaluable resource for discovering what more there is. Presumably the writer is not an idiot savant but knows more or less what is being produced. The reader joins the writer as co-author, bringing to light dimensions and depths of meaning often far transcending the conscious intention or deliberate design of the writer.

The recognition and even celebration of the role of the reader is a distinctive emphasis of contemporary literary theory and criticism. As Terry Eagleton suggests, "one might very roughly periodize the history of modern literary theory in three stages: a preoccupation with the actual historical writer (Romanticism and the nineteenth century); an exclusive concern with the text

(**New Criticism**); and a marked shift of attention to the reader over recent years. The reader has always been the most underprivileged of this trio—strangely, since without him or her there would be no literary texts at all" (1983, 74). But it is significant that, in 1991, Umberto Eco contends that, "in the course of the last few decades, the rights of the interpreters have been overstressed" (1991, 6). In any act of communication (including the reading of a literary text or the interpretation of an aesthetic work), there is an addresser as well as an addressee. Both are ineliminable. Both have their rights and their responsibilities. But is reading truly a life-and-death struggle in which the rights of the author-reader can be won only by destroying all vestiges of the (author-)writer? Or is it rather the exciting though difficult art of *cooperatively* making sense out of texts? And is it fair to exclude from this cooperative undertaking author-writers because they descend from a line that, in the past, claimed (or had thrust upon them) absolute sovereignty? Initially, the democratization of reading might require the execution of an entrenched class of noblemen (a.k.a. "authors" or "writers"); but the result of this process should be inclusiveness, the refusal to exclude arbitrarily any relevant party from participating in the production of meaning. So, the rebirth of the author need not pose any threat to the reader.

Author's intention or **authorial intention.** Usually used to suggest that the meaning of a text is primarily limited to what the author intended. William Wimsatt, Jr., and Monroe Beardsley in "The Intentional Fallacy," the manifesto of the so-called **New Criticism,** mounted a persuasive critique of this view. More recently, E. D. Hirsch, Jr., has tried to rehabilitate the notion of authorial intention.

Authority, method of. Expression used by Charles S. Peirce to identify one of four possible ways of trying to fix or establish **beliefs,** specifically, the method of appealing to some socially accredited authority.

Beliefs are, according to Peirce, **habits** of action. When these habits are disrupted, doubts result, and in the struggle to overcome doubt and to fix belief, an **inquiry** (or investigation) arises. One way to overcome doubt is by appealing to the authority of some person or community. This is, in essence, the method of authority. Inevitably, it is doomed to fail, since some people even in the most priest- or police-ridden societies will acquire "a wider sort of social feeling" (CP 5.381), a feeling prompting them to consult the experience and reflections of persons in other countries or ages. While the fixation of belief is something we do as participants in a community, no actual community can serve as the ultimate arbiter. As a way of fixing beliefs, Peirce's appeal to the community is an appeal to what an infinite or ideal community would reach in the long run, not to what some historical group happens to believe on the basis of finite experience. Thus he insists that "one man's experience is nothing, if it stands alone. If he sees what others cannot, we call it hallucination. It is not 'my' experience, but 'our' experience that has to be thought of; and this 'us' has indefinite possibilities" (CP 5.402n2). Any group narrower than this "we" is not considered to have the authority to fix beliefs rationally.

Auto-. A common prefix in English (from Greek) meaning *self* (for instance, autodidacts are those who have taught themselves—thus, self-teachers). Its opposite, *heter-* or *hetero-* (other), is also a common prefix in English (heterosexual, one who is attracted to members of the other or opposite sex).

Autocriticism, Autocritique. Self-criticism. See **heterocriticism.** Autocriticism is, according to Julia **Kristeva** and other contemporary semioticians, a distinctive feature of semiotic inquiry. For at every phase in its production or execution, such inquiry is compelled (in Kristeva's words) to think "of its object, its instrument and the relation between them." This makes of semiotics "an open form of research, a constant critique that turns back on itself and offers its own autocritique."

Autogenesis. Self-genesis or self-origin. Autogenesis is the process through which something gives rise to itself rather than being produced by an external agent or force.

Autonomy. In one sense, freedom; in another, somewhat peculiar, sense, a unique property of a literary work or, more generally, a semiotic system—the property of referring to itself. Roman **Jakobson** and others use this term to designate the self-referentiality of a literary work. *Autonymy* and *autoreflexivity* have also been used to identify this feature. The function of such works is not to refer to something beyond themselves (such as class struggle) but to reveal the structures and mechanisms of language, especially literary language. Indeed, any attempt to make a literary work refer to an extraliterary reality violates the integrity of the work. The insistence that autonomy, autonymy, or autoreflexivity defines literary texts is strenuously challenged by Marxists and other contextualists.

Autotelic. From the Greek *auto-* and *telos,* meaning self and goal or end. A process or practice having no other **function** or goal than itself. If you and I are conversing solely for the sake of the process of conversing, refusing to subordinate this delightful exchange to any outside goal, our conversation is autotelic. This term is ordinarily used to characterize the poetic use of language and, more

44

generally, the artistic use of any medium whatsoever. Hence, Roman **Jakobson** contends that an aesthetic message (for a loaded example, Archibald Macleish's poem "Ars Poetica") has no other function besides itself—that is, besides the ways in which it exploits and explores the possibilities inherent in some medium (language in the case of "Ars Poetica").

Auxiliant. A term eventually used by A. J. **Greimas** to identify a unit for the **analysis** of **narratives** by way of simplifying his original list of six **actants** (subject versus object; sender versus receiver; helper versus opponent). Greimas has more recently classified helper versus opponent as auxiliants.

Axiology. The study of values. The adjective *axiological* might mean that which pertains to the study of values or, more loosely, to values themselves.

Axiom. A term designating in traditional logic and mathematics an indemonstrable but, nonetheless, certain proposition. The truth of an axiom is often alleged to be *nota per se* (known through itself) rather than known through the truth of other propositions. In grasping the meaning of the proposition "A whole is greater than its parts" we also grasp its truth. While an axiom is a proposition whose truth is not derived from the truth of other propositions, it is itself a proposition from which other truths are derived. See also **postulate.**

Axis. A line around which a body or geometric figure rotates or may be supposed to rotate; more generally, a line around or along which something moves or on which it might be located.

In grade school we learned to imagine the earth rotating on its axis, this imaginary line proving helpful as a means of understanding how the earth both rotates around the sun and around itself. In **semiotics,** the distinct natures of **syntagmatic** and **paradigmatic** (or **associative**) relationships are often depicted along two distinct axes. Syntagmatic relationships occur among the various signifiers in a given utterance; these are part of a linear, temporal sequence in which the signifier heard at this moment replaces those just heard and, in its turn, will be eclipsed by those about to be heard. This sequence is conceived as moving along a horizontal axis. The relationships usually depicted along an intersecting vertical axis are what Ferdinand de **Saussure** called associative, today more commonly called paradigmatic relations. These occur among the signifier used and those others that might have been used instead. These relationships do not as such occur in time; at any moment, they make up an array of possibilities that overarches or accompanies the signifiers actually used. Just as it is useful to conceive the earth rotating around its imaginary axis, it is illuminating to consider utterances moving along (or located on) two distinct but intersecting axes.

B

Bakhtin, Mikhail (1895–1975). Russian philosopher and literary theorist whose writings bear upon a number of disciplines (linguistics, anthropology, philosophy, literary theory and criticism). Bakhtin's authorship is a problem for detectives, for he and others claim that he wrote works originally published under the names of colleagues. In his writings, indisputable and otherwise, a dialogical approach to language and literature is encountered.

Barthes, Roland (1915–1980). An extremely prolific French semiotician, essayist, and literary and cultural critic whose lively and engaging writings have been important in introducing semiology (or semiotics) to the United States. His books and essays make a significant and varied contribution to an understanding of (in Saussure's famous expression) "the life of signs within society." His books include *Writing Degree Zero* (1953), *Mythologies* (1957), *Critical Essays* (1964), *Elements of Semiology* (1964), *The Fashion System* (1967), *S/Z* (1970), *The Pleasure of the Text* (1973), *Image-Music-Text* (1977), and *The Semiotic Challenge* (1985).

One central feature of Barthes's thought is his adoption and use of Louis Hjelmslev's concept of **connotation** to explore a wide range of semiotic phenomena, including mass media, popular culture, style, fashion, literature, and photography. Another important aspect of his approach is the painstaking attention he devoted to identifying the various **codes** structuring literary texts. He maintained that "[t]he reluctance to declare its codes characterizes bourgeois society and the mass culture issuing from it: both demand signs which do not look like signs" (*Barthes Reader*, 287). Barthes took it as his task to expose these codes and, in a sense, destroy the power of these self-effacing signs by showing how they work. His concern was to demythologize the largely subliminal, and therefore powerful, "myths" by which those in control maintain their authority over society. Yet another influential aspect of his thought is the distinction between **readerly** (*lisible*) and **writerly** (*scriptible*) texts. Readerly texts are ones which leave the reader with "no more than the poor freedom either to accept or to reject the text": They are objects to be consumed rather than fabrics to be woven. In contrast, writerly texts are ones that clearly or effectively invite the reader to assume the role of authorship or co-authorship. Parallel to this distinction between writerly and readerly texts is Barthes's distinction between the writer (*scripteur, écrivant*) and the author (*écrivain*).

Barthes pursued the study of signs not so much as a discipline that might transform itself into a science as an instrument of cultural criticism. So do numerous other investigators of signs.

Bedeutung. German word ordinarily translated **reference,** as distinct from sense or **meaning (*Sinn*).** To use Gottlob Frege's famous example, "Morning Star" and "Evening Star" have the same reference (*Bedeutung*), since they both refer to the planet Venus; but the two expressions differ in their sense or meaning.

The term *meaning* is the source of no slight confusion in semiotics and countless other fields of inquiry (for instance, linguistics and philosophy). It is often used to cover both the sense and reference of words, expressions, or assertions; but it is also used in a narrower sense to mean sense or content, in contrast to reference.

Behaviorism. A psychological theory stressing (1) publicly observable and quantifiable dimensions of behavior, (2) the role of the environment in determining behavior, and (3) nurture (what is learned) over nature (what is innate or inborn). The most influential advocate of this psychological theory, B. F. Skinner, wrote a book titled *Verbal Behavior* in which he attempted to explain, strictly in behaviorist terms, the acquisition and use of language. The linguist Noam Chomsky and the literary figure Walker Percy have, in quite different ways, attacked Skinner's attempt to explain language in such terms. While

Chomsky stresses the innate capacity of human language users, Percy (following Charles S. **Peirce**) stresses the **triadic** character of human **semiosis.** For Percy, **dyadic** (two-termed) explanations of language, such as that offered by thinkers such as Skinner who recognize only publicly observable stimuli and responses to stimuli, are inadequate. Since semiosis is irreducibly triadic, such **reductionism** is misguided: Rather than explaining the operation of signs, it explains this phenomenon away, for behaviorism claims that there is nothing here to explain but the lawful correlations between stimulus and response. But for Percy, any theory that puts the utterances of human beings on a par with the peckings of pigeons thereby displays an impoverished sense of the complex reality (here, human language) it pretends to explain fully.

Behaviorist theory of meaning. An attempt to explain **meaning** in terms of the behavior of organisms in interaction with their environment. This environment includes other organisms of the same species; and, according to the behaviorist theory, the interaction of organisms belonging to the same species is the locus of meaning. In its primary sense, meaning is encountered not in the private thoughts, images, etc. of an isolated consciousness but in the public actions and reactions of environed organisms.

The behaviorist theory of meaning has been designed to challenge mentalist theories (attempts to explain meaning in terms of the contents or workings of mind or consciousness). One serious difficulty with this theory is its inability to explain—or, at best, its awkwardness in explaining—the common situation of comprehension taking place in the absence of behavior: A meaning is clearly grasped by an interpreter, but this comprehension does not prompt any behavioral reaction on the part of that interpreter. Hence it would seem that meaning cannot be simply identified with behavior. Charles S. **Peirce** and, to a far greater extent, Ludwig **Wittgenstein** have been influential in bringing to light the public or intersubjective character of meaning.

Being. A very general term used to designate whatever is, in whatever way; the status of being something rather than nothing. The nature and forms of being have been a pivotal preoccupation of Western thinkers. Questions regarding the relationship between being and representation (between the way things are in themselves and the way they are represented by means of **signs**) clearly fall within the scope of **semiotics**. See also **phenomenon, actuality, reality.**

Belief. In general, the conscious assent to the truth of a **proposition;** in Charles S. **Peirce,** a disposition (see **habit**) to act in certain ways in certain circumstances; that upon which a person is prepared to act.

Knowledge is sometimes defined in terms of belief (in one widely discussed definition, as justified, true belief). But belief is also contrasted with knowledge: Belief then means assent to the truth of a proposition based on the testimony or authority of another person, while knowledge means such assent on the basis of firsthand experience or one's own rational insight. If one cannot follow a complex argument but nonetheless accepts its conclusion because of one's confidence in a thinker who vouches for the conclusion, one *believes* the truth of the conclusion; if one can follow the argument and judges it to be valid, one *knows* this truth, for one's own rational insight—not one's trust in the competency of another—is the basis for assent.

Belief is, for Peirce, defined not in terms of **consciousness** but in terms of **habits** of action. Doubt results from the disruption of belief and, in turn, **inquiry** arises as the struggle to overcome doubt. To conceive belief, doubt, and inquiry in this way challenges the deeply ingrained tendency to locate them *in* a mind or consciousness separate from the world. Belief, doubt, and inquiry need to be understood in reference to the lives of embodied, situated agents, not disembodied, aloof minds (see **cogito**). **Pragmatism** flows quite naturally out of this definition of belief.

Benveniste, Emile (1902–1976). French linguist whose most important work is *Problems in General Linguistics* (1966). His contributions to semiotics include showing how language cannot be separated from either discourse or subjectivity. In Benveniste's linguistics, hence, we encounter an important challenge to the Saussurean project of studying *langue* (language) in abstraction from *parole* (**speech** or **discourse**) and from individual speakers or **subjects.** It is, for Benveniste, only in and through language that we constitute ourselves as subjects. This contention suggests an affinity between his thought and that of such thinkers as Jacques **Lacan,** Julia **Kristeva,** and Luce **Irigaray.**

Besprochen Welt. German expression used by Harald Weinrich and often translated as the discoursed or commented world, in contrast to the narrated world (*erzahlten Welt*). The *discoursed* world is one in which the **addresser** and **addressee** are directly involved; it is the textual world of the political memorandum, the critical essay, the lyric poem, and the scientific report. The *narrated* world is, in contrast, one in which addresser and addressee are not—or, at least, do not appear to be—co-present in the same world.

Binarism. The tendency to view topics or phenomena, even complex ones, in terms of oppositional pairs and aggregates of such pairs. See also **binary opposition.**

Binary code. A code (or set of correlations) based on two elementary **signals,** for example, the dot and dash of the Morse code or a negative and positive electrical impulse. Binarization is, thus, the process by which the elementary signals of one code (for example, the letters in the English alphabet) are translated into those of a binary code (A = 00000; B = 00001; C = 00010; etc.). The amount of information (that is, the number of units from the binary code) required for such a translation is described in terms of bits. It takes five bits of information to translate the twenty-six letters of the English alphabet.

Binary opposition. The opposition of two things; the state or process in which two things oppose each other. Often a binary opposition is understood as a pair of terms in which one is privileged (for example, male vs. female in the phallocentric discourses of Western culture).

Opposition is (as the Latin prefix *op-,* meaning against, itself suggests) an affair in which two things stand against each other. But even this simple characterization can be misleading because it might be taken to suggest that two self-contained and self-defined entities collide or exert pressure on one another. But, with **structuralism** and even other approaches, it is by means of oppositions that the very identities of some things are formed. This is what Ferdinand de **Saussure** meant when he asserted that "*In language there are only differences* [or oppositions]." Even more important than that is the fact that, although in general a difference presupposes positive terms between which the difference holds [or the opposition occurs], in a language there are only differences, *"and no positive terms."*

For the investigation of linguistic and other types of **signs,** opposition in general and binary opposition in particular are important. Such opposition makes possible **articulation** and thus **signification** (the process by which signs and meanings are generated). It is only by a thing standing over against other things that it stands out at all; and it is only by standing out that a thing marks itself off from other things. In short, opposition makes differentiation possible and, in turn, differentiation makes articulation possible. Take the words on this page. At the most basic level, they attain the status of being discernible signs by standing over against the page itself. Ink the same color as the page would be useless, for marks made with such ink would not stand out at all. The marks against a contrasting page are (in the language of **Gestalt** psychology) figures on a ground. Above this level, there is the differentiation of the marks from one another. Such differentiation also depends largely, if not solely, on a complex series of binary oppositions. This is most easily understood in terms of aural signs. The **phoneme** /pin/ is distinguishable from that of /tin/ solely by virtue of the sound of the initial consonant (the contrast or opposition between /p/ and /t/).

Frequently binary oppositions have been conceived in a hierarchical way, with one member of the pair construed as higher or of greater value than the other. In Western thought, some important binary oppositions have been matter/spirit; body/soul; emotion/reason; outward sign/ inward meaning; exterior/interior; surface/depth; margin/ central; appearance/reality; representation/presence; artificial/natural (nomos/physis). Traditionally, the second term in each pair has been **privileged** and the first term denigrated (matter is lower than spirit; body is lower than soul, emotion than reason, etc.). **Deconstruction,** an important trend in contemporary criticism (literary and philosophical), has challenged many, if not all, of these traditional hierarchies. One emphasis of deconstructive criticism is that there is no neutral ground upon which to launch such a critique, to challenge the rigidly fixed hierarchies of such traditional discourses as philosophy, theology, literature, etc. Such a critique can be initiated and sustained only in the very discourses and languages defined by such hierarchies. In other words, deconstructionist critics are themselves always already implicated in the very structures that they are challenging. For example, to try to shift the focus from what has traditionally been central to what has been marginal or peripheral (say, *from* literature as a process holding a mirror up to humankind *to* literature conceived as a richly textured fabric, in continuous process of being woven and unwoven) reinforces in certain ways the traditional hierarchy of center/margin. See also **dualism.**

Biosemiosis. From *bio-*, life, and *semiosis,* sign action. The sign processes found among living things; this term encompasses **anthroposemiosis, zoosemiosis,** and (conceivably, at least) **phytosemiosis.**

Biosemiotics. The study of the sign processes in the biosphere or world of living things. It includes **anthroposemiotics, zoosemiotics,** and (in the judgment of some semioticians) **phytosemiotics.**

Bit. A technical term in information theory meaning the elementary unit of information measurement, of how many elementary **signals** of a **binary code** are needed to translate the elementary units of a more complex code (for example, the English alphabet). The English alphabet can be translated into a binary code using no more than five bits of information (A = 00000; B = 00001; C = 00010; D = 00011; E = 00100; etc.).

Bliss (*jouissance*), texts of. A type of text identified by Roland **Barthes** and contrasted to texts of pleasure (*plaisir*). A text of pleasure is one "that contents, fills, grants euphoria; the text that comes from culture and does not break with it, is linked to a *comfortable* practice of reading." In contrast, a text of bliss is one "that imposes a state of loss, the text that discomforts (perhaps to the point of a certain boredom), unsettles the reader's historical, cultural, psychological assumptions, the consistency of his tastes, values, memories, brings to a crisis his relation with language" (1973 [1975], 14). Texts of pleasure are objects to be consumed, while ones of bliss are like persons with whom you make love.

Barthes's objective in drawing this distinction is to suggest that, when texts are properly approached, there is both an erotics and a politics of reading. Reading involves something analogous to seduction, foreplay, and even orgasm; *jouissance* is the term he uses because (among other things) it signifies the bliss one experiences during orgasm. Reading also involves transgression, rebellion, and defiance. In the spirit of rebellion characteristic of the late 1960s and early 1970s, Barthes proclaimed that "[t]he text is (or should be) that uninhibited person who shows his behind to the *Political Father*" (1973 [1975], 53). The erotics of reading requires that the unique "texture" of the text be experienced for its own sake, an activity that propels readers toward bliss but along the way exposes them to all the risks inherent in eros. The politics of reading requires the courage to make one or another obscene gesture to the institutionalized authorities that would control meanings and package messages.

Bricolage. A term introduced by Claude Levi-Strauss (1908–) to designate the manner in which the so-called savage or primitive mind orients itself to the world, in particular to natural objects and events on the one hand and to social beings and their interactions on the other. What distinguishes this manner is its reliance upon improvisational (or **ad hoc**) and makeshift responses, as well as far-flung analogies (for example, totemism). These analogies strike the "civilized" mind (the mind of those shaped by literacy and technology) as far-fetched as well as far-flung. But such a judgment is all too likely an excuse for missing the logic inherent in the way nonliterate, nontechnological cultures orient themselves to the objects and events encountered in the course of life. The makeshift tinkerer or handyman (the **bricoleur**) is no less logical or rational in his approach than is the highly trained engineer. Rather than condemning or dismissing the approach exemplified in "primitive" cultures, Levi-Strauss wanted to explain this. His conception of bricolage and its basis in the image of the bricoleur are central to this undertaking.

Bricoleur. Tinkerer; handyman. The structuralist anthropologist Claude Levi-Strauss devised his important and influential conception of **bricolage** from the characteristic manner in which a handyman works. This manner involves, above all, tinkering with this and that, not being too concerned with overall consistency but finely attentive to some immediate situation. It also involves using whatever materials and tools are available. This manner is, in short, makeshift. It contrasts sharply with that of the characteristic way highly specialized engineers work, for such technological specialists routinely devise special tools and create new materials as part of their work (for instance, building a space shuttle). The mind of "primitive" persons is more like that of a bricoleur, while the mind of "civilized" persons (persons shaped by literacy and technology) is more like that of an engineer. It is not that "primitive" people are illogical or unreasonable; rather it is that their logic (or form of rationality) is best conceived not in terms of the engineer's but of the bricoleur's modus operandi.

Buchler, Justus (1914–1991). A **contemporary** American philosopher who articulated a general theory of human judgment having direct though still largely overlooked relevance to the study of signs. His distinction of the three modes of judgment—assertive, active, and exhibitive—and also his explorations of art and, in particular, poetry as a form of exhibitive judgment merit serious attention. His rigorous and nuanced discussions of such topics as meaning, communication, and query deserve the same. The titles of greatest relevance here are *Charles Peirce's Empiricism* (1939), *Nature and Judgment* (1955), *Toward a General Theory of Human Judgment* (1951; revised edition 1979), *The Concept of Method* (1961), *The Main of Light: On the Concept of Poetry* (1974).

Buhler, Karl (1879–1963). German psychologist who devoted considerable attention to language and expression. One of his specific contributions is the principle of dominance, which states that while every **message** may have several **functions,** ordinarily only one is predominant. The results of his studies can be found in *Ausdruckstheorie* (1933) and *Sprachtheorie* (1935). Though Charles S. **Peirce** carefully distinguished the general theory of **signs** from psychology, he encouraged psychologists to investigate human sign-making and sign-using functions.

C

CA. Conversation analysis.

Canon. A body of writings recognized as authoritative or exemplary. Today there is an important controversy regarding how canons are established, maintained, and revisable.

Cartesian, Cartesianism. From *Cartesius*, the Latin form of Descartes; related to the philosophy of the early **modern** French philosopher René **Descartes** (1596–1650), whose writings present a self-conscious rebellion against medieval thought. *Cartesian* is often used in a more general sense to designate the position of someone who is committed to the primacy of subjectivity, or the quest for absolute certainty, or immediate (or intuitive) knowledge, or any combination of these commitments.

Descartes is considered by many the father of modern philosophy. As Richard J. Bernstein has suggested, this title is best taken in a Freudian sense; for, starting early on, his "sons" have been trying to kill him off. This can clearly be seen in the case of Charles S. **Peirce.** His philosophical authorship virtually began with a critique of Descartes. In a series of articles published in the late 1860s, Peirce in one stroke attacked Cartesianism and laid the foundation for his general theory of signs. In particular, he rejected the doctrine of immediate or intuitive knowledge (see **immediate knowledge, intuition**) and the authority of the isolated individual or consciousness (Descartes's **cogito**). All knowledge is, according to Peirce, mediated by signs; moreover, it is acquired not by retreating into the cloister of one's own consciousness but by participating in the rough-and-tumble of communal inquiry. See also **dialogism; intersubjectivity; subjectivity, primacy of.**

Cassirer, Ernst (1874–1945). German philosopher who taught at a number of universities, including Berlin, Hamburg, Oxford, Yale, and Columbia. *Language and Myth* (1925), *Symbol, Myth, and Culture* (1935), *An Essay on Man* (1944), and the three volumes of *The Philosophy of Symbolic Forms* (1923, 1925, 1929) are especially relevant to the study of sign. Cassirer defined human beings as *animal symbolicum* (the symbol-using animal). The semiotic cast of his thought is also suggested in his contention that "[t]he sign is no mere accidental cloak of the idea, but is necessary and essential organ . . ." (1923, 86). For Cassirer, myth, art, religion, science, and history taken together make up a complex world of symbolic forms but each one of these in itself exhibits its own distinctive symbols and symbolic laws.

Categoreal (also **categorical**) **scheme.** A set of **categories** by which data are organized or interpreted. One way to conceive the mind has been as a mass of largely formless, inert stuff upon which objects and events impress themselves. Another way has been to see the mind as an inherently structured, dynamic organ. A categoreal scheme is, thus, the set of principles by which the mind structures or organizes its data. To speak of a scheme, however, is to stress not the categories in isolation from one another but the interconnection of the categories; that is, the way these principles of organization work together.

Categories. The most universal concepts or ideas; the ultimate genera (plural of genus); more loosely, general ideas by which one grasps some aspect of reality or some feature of experience.

In the history of Western philosophy, **Plato, Aristotle,** Kant, Hegel, and **Peirce** each devoted considerable attention to articulating a doctrine of categories. Since Aristotle's list of categories is the closest to common sense, it serves well as an illustration. Aristotle's categories are substance, quantity, quality, relation, place, time, position, state, action, and affection (or passion). For Aristotle, anything whatsoever can be subsumed under one of these categories (for example, kinship belongs under the category of relationship, weight under that of quantity, and yesterday under that of time). In the *Critique of Pure Reason,* Immanuel Kant criticized the Aristotelian categories for being a mere rhapsody, for Aristotle (at least in his extant writings) offers little in the way of explaining how he derived these categories or why he is justified in elevating these conceptions to the status of categories. Starting with Kant, the related problems of deriving and justifying the categories have been central concerns of virtually all thinkers who address this topic.

Categories, Peircean. Firstness (in-itselfness), **secondness** (over-againstness), and **thirdness** (in-betweenness); or, stated alternatively, qualitative immediacy, brute opposition, and dynamic mediation.

Peirce's categories were designed to call attention to what he supposed were the ever-present features or aspects of any **phenomenon** whatsoever. Whatever comes before the mind is, in some ways, ineffable (what it uniquely is in itself eludes the possibility of being communicated), insistent (whatever comes before the mind also stands over against the mind: It insists upon itself in opposition to others), and intelligible (it can be noted and named and even, to some extent, interpreted or explained). Charles S. **Peirce**'s categories of firstness, secondness, and thirdness are, at once, the most important (because they so deeply inform and guide his investigation of signs) and the most difficult of his ideas.

One of the functions of Peirce's categories is to guide and stimulate **inquiry.** They are, in a word, **heuristic.** This is evident in the way the categories are used by Peirce in his exploration of the various types of signs. Any sign can be taken as something *in itself*; it might also be considered in relation *to another* (its object); finally, a sign might function as a go-between (a factor mediating between its object and its interpretant). From this threefold consideration, Peirce derives three trichotomies: First: **qualisign, sinsign, legisign.** Second: **icon, index, symbol.** Third: **rheme, dicent, argument.**

Cathexis. A psychoanalytic term designating an excitatory or urging force within the psyche, in contrast to an anticathexis (an inhibitory or checking force). According to Sigmund Freud, a psychoanalytic approach to our mental life focuses on the complex interplay of cathexes and anticathexes; that is, of excitatory and inhibitory forces.

Channel. A term sometimes used as a synonym for contact. In any process of **communication,** there must be a channel or contact—some physical or actual connection between the **addresser** and **addressee** (the sender and recipient) of a message. An example of this would be the wire linking one telephone to another.

Chora. From the Greek word for receptacle. A term borrowed by Julia **Kristeva** from Plato's *Timaeus* denoting

61

"an essentially mobile and extremely provisional articulation constituted by movements and their ephemeral states" (1974 [1984], 25). The chora "precedes evidence, verisimilitude, spatiality, and temporality. Our discourse—all discourse—moves with and against the chora in the sense that it simultaneously depends upon and refuses it" (26). What Kristeva is trying to capture here cannot, in principle, be captured: It is the *ineffable* dimension of discourse. It corresponds, at least roughly, to what Charles S. **Peirce** calls firstness, an immediacy that "precedes all synthesis and all differentiation; it has not unity and not parts. It cannot be articulately thought: Assert it, and it has already lost its characteristic innocence. . . . Stop to think of it, and it has flown" (CP 1.357).

Cinema. An important and interesting field of contemporary semiotic research. Just as the semiotics of cinema has become a major trend in contemporary film theory, so film or cinema has become a lively topic of semiotic research today. Here we can see the intersection and crossfertilization of what thirty years ago were independent research traditions. The semiotic explorations of cinema undertaken by Christian Metz, Pier Paolo Pasolini, Teresa de Lauretis, Kaja Silverman, and the equally ubiquitous Roland **Barthes** and Umberto **Eco** are especially noteworthy. See also **suture**.

Clarity, grades of. Distinct levels or grades of conceptual clearness concerning the **signs** we are using. In what is likely his best-known writing, "How to Make Our Ideas Clear," Charles S. **Peirce** distinguished three grades of clarity: subjective familiarity, abstract definition, and pragmatic clarification.

At the most basic level, a person might exhibit subjective familiarity with a sign by being able to use or interpret the sign appropriately. When I tried to convince my five-year-old son that when I was his age I rode a dinosaur to school, he responded by claiming that this narrated event never took place (in his own words, "That's not real"). His use of "real" here exhibits a familiarity, a genuine but rudimentary level of comprehension. It is, however, unlikely that he could formulate an abstract definition of what he and others mean—or ought to mean—by the term "real." The capacity to produce such a definition (for example, the real is that which is independent of what you or I or any other finite individual or actual group of such individuals happens to think) indicates a grade of clarity higher than that of familiarity. But there is, according to Peirce, a level of clarity above that of abstract definition; this level is attained by means of the pragmatic maxim (see **pragmatism**).

According to this maxim, we should frame our conceptions in terms of their conceivable practical effects (that is, in terms of their possible bearing upon human conduct). The conception of God as a being worthy of adoration, reverence, and worship would amount to a pragmatic clarification, for it defines God explicitly in terms of what conduct is appropriate (adoration, reverence, worship). The primary purpose of Peirce's pragmatic maxim is to push our inquiries to a grade of clarity higher than that of abstract definition. Of course, whether there really *is* such a being is a question regarding the truth of the claim that there is a God. Peirce's maxim is designed to deal directly with questions not of truth but of meaning. First, we must know what we are talking about; then and only then can we determine the reliability of our claims or the truth of our judgments. To be clear about what we mean by an idea is in itself no warrant for attributing existence or **reality** to the object (the *ens rationis*) conceived through this idea.

Clôture. The conceptual limits inherent in a **problematique** in which one is involved or in a **paradigm** to which an investigator is committed. A *problématique* or paradigm not only orients research; it also constrains it along certain paths. *Cloture* designates those constraints, usually unnoticed until after a **coupure epistemologique** or **paradigm shift.**

Code. One of the six factors involved in any communicative process. Corresponding to this factor is the **metalinguistic** (or metalingual) **function.** When **communication** is oriented toward the code or codes upon which it depends, its function is said to be metalinguistic (or, since the system of signs might not be a language except in a very loose or metaphorical sense, metasemiotic). Ordinarily, in conveying messages, we make use of codes; occasionally the message turns toward and concerns the code itself. If you are told that the hand gesture meaning "OK" in Anglo-American settings is an obscene gesture in Brazil the message is metalinguistic, since it is directed to calling attention to a code.

In semiotic texts, two senses of code are encountered most frequently. In one sense, code means a set of rules prescribing how to act or what to do, and in another, a key (or set of instructions) for translating a message. Morse code is a key for correlating particular patterns of clicks and silences to letters of the alphabet. Codes as sets of rules are normative: They provide us the norms to judge whether we are acting appropriately. Judgments of mispronunciation are only possible in reference to the codification of sounds found in an alphabet. Of course, not all violations of a code signal ineptitude or incompetence; some result from deliberate or conscious decision—for example, when a person desiring to shock people shows up on a formal occasion dressed in a bathing suit, thereby breaking the fashion code. This example suggests an important distinction: A code need not be explicitly formulated. In fact, most codes might be sets of more or less implicit (or unstated) rules: They are acquired through imitative behavior and are followed, in a sense, unconsciously.

Roland **Barthes** and Umberto **Eco** are two contemporary semioticians who have devoted considerable attention to codes. Their investigations are especially important for showing that, in most contexts of communication, more than one code is at work and also that, for an understanding of works of art, attention to the violation or transgression of codes is imperative.

Coenoscopic. A term used by Jeremy Bentham and adopted by Charles S. **Peirce** to designate the range of observations open to virtually any human inquirer. Derived from Greek: The prefix (*coeno-*) means common and the root (*scopic*) to observe. Some forms of inquiry (most notably philosophy) are, according to Peirce, coenoscopic: They appeal to such observations as come within the range of every human being's normal experience in every waking hour of their lives. In contrast, other investigations (such as physics and chemistry) are idioscopic: They depend upon focused observation often aided by special training and/or technology. The distinction between coenoscopic and idioscopic types of inquiry is not intended to separate philosophy from science. Quite the contrary; it shows just what kind of science philosophy is. Philosophy's status as a science and its very aspiration for this status have been, of course, questioned and challenged. But Peirce's claim here is quite modest: When he contends that philosophy is either science or it is balderdash, he simply means that it must strive to be a communal, empirical form of inquiry—one whose conclusions are established by ongoing appeals to the daily experience of human beings.

Cogito. Latin word meaning "I think": *Cogito ergo sum* ("I think, therefore I am"). *Cogito* is a term taken from the **modern** French philosopher René **Descartes**'s writings and used to designate the **"I,"** in particular the "I" as thinker. It is also a symbol for the primacy of subjectivity, of the perspective that the "I" is original and that all else (in particular, the world and language) is derivative. Since Descartes did not acknowledge the unconscious, the term *cogito* is often used to designate the self as a being both unified and transparent to itself. Recent theories of subjectivity (such as those of Jacques **Lacan,** Julia **Kristeva,** and Luce **Irigaray**) stress just the opposite— the self as a divided being (conscious/unconscious) and as one largely opaque to itself. Also, Descartes did not appreciate the importance of language, especially as a factor in what has been called the **engendering of subjectivity.** The "I" is, after all, a being who can call itself such, who can use language *reflexively:* The capacity for self-identification, self-description, self-reference, etc. is essential for what is generally designated as subjectivity. But this capacity is linguistic; as Emile **Benveniste** observes, it is only in and through language that we constitute ourselves as subjects. While contemporary theories of subjectivity emphasize language, Descartes ignored its importance. In sum, *cogito* is, to many contemporary semioticians, the name for a mistake—or set of mistakes—from which we still have not fully extricated ourselves.

Collective mind. Both the sociologist Emile Durkheim and the linguist Ferdinand de **Saussure** supposed that, over and above individual minds, there is a collective mind. This is not a mere aggregate of individual minds but something not reducible to them. The supposition that there is a collective mind is controversial, especially in Anglo-American contexts where methodological individualism tends to be the prevailing view. According to this view, only individuals are real and anything supposedly other than individuals (for example, society or culture) is reducible to what individuals undergo, do, think, and feel. But, Durkheim, Saussure, and countless other thinkers have insisted that individuals in interaction with one another display properties not exhibited by individuals in isolation. In addition, they stress that the bias of methodological individualism forces us to overlook the subtle but actual ways in which social constraints and forces, operating beneath the level of individual consciousness and beyond the control of individual volition, actually shape the experiences, actions, thoughts, and even feelings of individuals.

Collective unconscious. Carl **Jung** proposed that, in addition to the personal unconscious (that region of the human psyche having its origin largely in the repression of experiences actually undergone by an individual in the course of life), there is a collective unconscious. This is the repository of our "racial," rather than individual, experiences: What the human race has undergone in its actual evolution has, in some measure and manner, become encoded in the human organism itself, such that instincts and **archetypes** are transmitted from earlier generations to later ones. The supposition that there is a collective unconscious is a highly controversial one; but it is a position for which Jung strenuously and painstakingly argued, not entirely without effect.

Communication. The process of transmitting and receiving a **message**. According to Roman Jakobson and others, an analysis of this process yields six factors:

addresser, addressee, contact (or **channel**), **context, code,** and the message itself. Corresponding to these factors are six functions: emotive, **conative, phatic, reference, metalinguistic** (or metacommunicative), and aesthetic or poetic.

This process has been taken as the focal object of semiotics. For example, Roman **Jakobson** proposed that "[t]he subject matter of semiotics is the communication of any messages whatsoever, whereas the field of linguistics is confined to the communication of **verbal** messages." In addition, Margaret Mead defined semiotics as the study of "patterned communication in all modalities."

Competence and **performance.** Competence, a set of capacities enabling the execution of a task; performance, the execution itself. This distinction was drawn by the linguist Noam Chomsky and has been widely adopted by semioticians as well as linguists.

The distinction between competence and performance corresponds at least roughly to *langue* and *parole,* for *langue* is the system that makes communication possible and *parole* is the use to which the system is concretely put. The possession of a competency does not entail the exhibition of that competency: A person might be a competent user of English without, at this moment, using it. The distinction between competence and performance suggests two distinct and (for some) separable fields of inquiry. On the one hand, we might explore the conditions underlying a given competency (say the ability to speak and understand English); on the other hand, we might investigate specific performances (such as verbal and nonverbal communication between lovers), paying little or no attention to the general conditions underlying these performances. Like Ferdinand de **Saussure**'s attempt to separate the study of *langue* from that of *parole*, attempts to isolate investigations of competencies from those of performances are ultimately doomed to fail, even though there is a legitimate distinction to be drawn between competence and performance.

Conative. The adjective used to designate one of the six basic functions of a communicational exchange, namely the function of such an exchange when it is oriented or directed toward the **addressee.** One and the same message might be either emotive or conative. If, for example, I say that "I'm tired" simply to inform you of my state, then the message is, in a way, oriented toward the speaker or **addresser** and is emotive. If, however, the force of my utterance in this **context** is "Let's go home," then the predominant function of the message is conative, for it is not so much a revelation about me as a request to you. Grammatically, imperative or vocative expressions ("Open the window" and "O Lord, I beseech thee," respectively) most clearly illustrate the conative function.

Conclusion. The statement in an argument for which evidence is presented. The statements put forth as evidence for the conclusion are called premises.

Condensation. A psychoanalytic term (see **psychoanalysis**) for the mental process whereby the unconscious telescopes or condenses several latent meanings into one manifest element (see **latent** vs. **manifest content**). In condensation, we encounter the formation of a new **signifier** from the fusion of what in other contexts or at an earlier time were distinct or even separate signifiers. Jacques **Lacan** identifies **metaphor** with the process of condensation and **metonymy** with that of **displacement.**

Connotation. A term meaning the associations (often emotionally charged) surrounding a word, in contrast

69

to its denotation, its precise or strict meaning. In semiotic writings, connotation means a secondary or derived meaning, while denotation signifies the primary or first meaning of a sign. This sense of connotation is central to Roland **Barthes**'s semiology. **Meaning** results whenever a signifier is correlated with a signified. Imagine an ad involving a photograph of a young, attractive woman sitting on the shoulders of a male companion, both obviously enjoying themselves on a beach in Florida. The photo is the signifier, the couple is the signified. But more is going on in this photo than the depiction of two people: A message is being conveyed, one about where and how to have fun. It is, after all, an ad for a spring fling aimed at college students. The correlation of this couple and this photographic image is called by many semioticians the plane (or level) of denotation; the correlation of this with the message "Fun-in-the-sun" is called the plane of connotation.

A third meaning of connotation is used in **logic.** Again, it is contrasted with denotation; but here, connotation is the meaning of a word or expression and the denotation the reference (the range of objects to which the word or expression refers). "Planet" *means,* or connotes, a body of rather considerable size revolving around the sun; it *refers to,* or denotes, the actual bodies fitting this description: Mercury, Venus, Mars, Earth, etc. You can discover what "planet" connotes by looking in a dictionary; you need a telescope and other instruments to find out what it denotes.

Consciousness. A synonym for awareness; also the capacity of an organism to respond to or at least to note intra- and extrasomatic events and objects.

According to Charles S. **Peirce,** "whenever we think,

we have present to . . . [our] consciousness some feeling, image, conception, or other representation, which serves as a **sign**" (CP 5.328). This suggests that consciousness is a fabric of signs. Here, as in so many other contexts, we see that the value of a truly general theory of signs is that it invites us to interpret anew topics such as consciousness, knowledge, and **subjectivity.** Beyond this, it provides us with the resources for doing so.

Constative. J. L. **Austin**'s name for statements about which it is appropriate to ask whether they are true or false (for example, "The cat is on the mat").

Austin was especially interested in calling attention to **performative utterances** (utterances about which it does not make any sense to ask whether they are true or false, for instance, "I baptize this child Peter Carlo" uttered by a minister in the actual circumstances of a baptismal ceremony). Performative utterances may go wrong in one way or another (for example, when I place a bid at an auction I may do so in an inappropriate way and, thereby, negate the validity of my utterance); but they can be neither true nor false. Ultimately, Austin was interested in challenging the simplistic ways in which we have traditionally thought about language. See also **nomenclature.**

Conspicuous consumption. In *The Theory of the Leisure Class* (1899), Thorstein Veblen called attention to the phenomenon of consuming goods and services not as a means of satisfying needs but as a way of communicating status and wealth. This suggests that an adequate understanding of commodities must draw upon **semiotics** as well as economics. What a consumer society produces, above all else, are consumers; and, as much as anything else, these are consumers of signs. So when we see a person wearing a shirt bearing *Gucci,* it seems appropriate to ask whether the shirt or the wearer is the product.

Contact. See **channel.**

Contemporary. A term often used by philosophers and historians of ideas in contrast to the adjective **modern.** Modern means postmedieval (the Middle Ages or **medieval** period, stretching roughly from A.D. 500–1500) and precontemporary. The beginning of the contemporary era is a matter of dispute. Sometimes it is defined in terms of the German philosopher Georg Wilhelm Friedrich Hegel (1770–1831), since many of the most important nineteenth-century and even early-twentieth-century movements in philosophy (existentialism, Marxism, **pragmatism,** and analytic philosophy) were in some measure a reaction against Hegel. So defined, contemporary means post-Hegelian. Sometimes the beginning is taken to be the late nineteenth or early twentieth century. René **Descartes** (1596–1650) and Immanuel Kant (1724–1804) are modern thinkers, whereas John **Dewey** (1859–1952), Martin Heidegger (1889–1976), and Ludwig **Wittgenstein** (1889–1951) are **contemporary.**

Though it can draw on a long and rich history, semiotics—understood as a general theory of signs conscious of its distinct and (to some extent) autonomous status—is a contemporary development.

Content and expression. A distinction introduced by Louis Hjelmslev and corresponding at least roughly to Saussure's distinction between **signified** and **signifier.** At the heart of any sign, one finds (according to Hjelmslev) a correlation between an expression plane and a content plane. These are two distinguishable but inseparable aspects of the sign: The plane of the signifiers is the expression plane and that of the signifieds is the content plane.

Context. The circumstance or situation in which a **message** is transmitted and received. Context is one of the six most basic factors in any process of **communication.** The other factors are **addresser, addressee,** contact (or **channel**), **code,** and the message itself. Corresponding to **context** is the referential function of communication. When I warn a friend of an onrushing car by shouting "Look out!" the communication is oriented toward the context; in such cases, the referential function is predominant. See **Co-text.**

Contextualism. An emphasis on the importance or indispensability of viewing a sign process in light of the context or contexts in which the process occurs. Of course, context might be construed in broader or narrower ways. For example, one might take the context of a novel to be the immediate circumstances in which it was written, or one might take the context to be a significant portion of literary history (specifically, say, the nineteenth-century novel). A contextualist approach is distinct from, and often opposed to, a **formalist** approach. The formalist stresses the autonomous and self-contained character of a sign process (text, discourse, etc.), in effect removing it from its context.

Continuity, continuum. Continuity, the state or character of being continuous or uninterrupted; continuum, an uninterrupted sequence or unbroken development. Charles S. **Peirce** stressed the need to treat apparently disparate **phenomena** as though they were points on the same continuum. See also **synechism.**

Convention. From Latin *convenire,* to come together. An established practice or **usage.** *Conventional* and *arbitrary* are often used interchangeably. But greater care should be taken in how these words are used. Among the established (that is, conventional) meanings of *arbitrary,* two deserve attention here: In one sense, this term means that which is dependent on the will; in another, that which is without reason. These two senses do not necessarily coincide, for something may be dependent on my will but, at the same time, quite rational or reasonable—for instance, the success of a campaign to recycle cans and bottles.

All conventions or established practices are arbitrary in the first sense; they depend on our willingness to continue doing the thing that has customarily been done. Apart from this willingness, they would disappear. But conventions are not necessarily without reason or justification, even if it is not evident to us what this justification is. The established practice of greeting one another civilly might have a deep though unappreciated warrant. The fate of this convention depends upon us. This does not make the convention unreasonable, only fragile.

Convention has traditionally been contrasted with nature. The contrast between *nomos* (custom) and *phusis* (nature) championed by, above all, Plato and Aristotle, set a pattern for much later thought. For both of these ancient Greek philosophers, the appeal to nature was decisive. As in so many other respects, **contemporary** thought diverges on this point sharply from the dominant thrust of classical thought, for contemporary thought contains a challenge to the privileging of nature and the denigration of custom. For most people today, all appeals to nature are problematic, for they know all too well how such appeals have been used to justify slavery and other forms of exploitation or oppression. In sum, a sense of historical contingency has replaced one of natural finality.

Conventional signs. Signs based upon a **convention**

and contrasted with natural signs. A young girl observes a rapidly darkening sky and takes it to be a sign of an approaching storm. As she is frantically looking for her dog, she hears her aunt calling her name. Traditionally, the storm clouds are an example of natural signs, while names and other words an example of conventional signs.

Conversation/inquiry. Today the metaphor of conversation, largely through the influence of Richard Rorty, has assumed an importance and even centrality that it previously did not have. According to Rorty, philosophers should cease seeing philosophy as a form of **inquiry** (a process of **semiosis** aimed at the discovery of truth and thereby committed to the convergence of perspectives) and begin to see it simply as a part of the conversation of humankind. In addition, philosophers should not presume the authority to tell others (that is, other disciplines) what they mean or how they should proceed. Philosophy is not the ultimate arbiter of the human conversation; it is but one voice among others and not necessarily either the most important or the most authoritative voice.

Conversational rules. In an influential essay entitled "Logic and Conversation," Paul Grice argued that certain rules should guide any conversational exchange committed to the cooperative principle. This principle enjoins participants in conversation to do the following: "Make your conversational contribution such as is required, at the stage at which it occurs, by the accepted purpose or direction of the talk exchange in which you are engaged" (1989, 26). From this principle, Grice derives four categories of rules or maxims—quantity, quality, relation, and manner. Quantity concerns the amount of information to be conveyed by any participant in conversation; under this heading fall, above all else, two maxims: "Make your contribution as informative as is required, for the current purpose of the exchange" and "Do not make your contribution more informative than is required." Quality concerns the quality or reliability of the information being conveyed. Under it falls the supermaxim—"Try to make your contribution one that is true"—and under this supermaxim fall above all two more specific directives: "Do not say what you believe to be false" and "Do not say that for which you lack adequate evidence." Under the category of relation falls the injunction "Be relevant" and under that of manner the supermaxim "Be perspicuous." Under the requirement of perspicuity fall, of course, a variety of maxims (the most important being "Avoid obscurity," "Avoid ambiguity," "Be brief," and "Be orderly"). Since Grice himself seems to spend more words than needed to state the rules of conversation, it is likely that he violates his own requirement of quantity.

Conversation analysis (CA). CA is an empirical, inductive investigation, ordinarily undertaken by sociolinguists and social psychologists, devoted to examining actual conversations primarily by means of recordings and audio/video tapes. Conversation analysis should not be confused with **discourse analysis,** the latter being characteristically a formal, deductive inquiry rather than an empirical, inductive investigation.

Cooperative principle. See **conversational rules.**

Co-text. A term sometimes used to designate the **verbal** or **semiotic** environment of some semiotic process or practice, in contrast to its extraverbal (or extrasemiotic) **context.** This latter is sometimes called the situational environment. Take a simple example. This entry on co-text occurs in the co-text of this glossary: It is a text embedded in a larger text. But both of these texts—the single entry and the entire glossary—are part of a world that is made up of more than words. This world, especially those features of it to which the statements in this book pertain, is the extraverbal environment.

Coupure épistémologique. **Epistemological** rupture or shift. A sudden, usually unsettling transition from one **problématique** (or complex of problems) to another. In literary theory and criticism, the shift from a psycho-biographical approach to a structuralist approach would be—and, in fact, is—a *coupure epistemologique*. This term designates what in Anglo-American discourse is called a **paradigm shift.**

Critic. A branch of **logic** as conceived by Charles S. **Peirce.** Critic (occasionally called critical logic) is the branch concerned with the various forms of **argument.** Eventually Peirce came to conceive logic as a tripartite discipline: Its first part, **speculative grammar,** is concerned with the processes and forms of meaning (these are sign-actions and sign-types); the second part, critic, is devoted to the processes and forms of **inference;** and the third, **speculative rhetoric** or **methodeutic,** a theory of **inquiry.** Ordinarily logic is limited to what Peirce called critic, so his conception of this discipline is broader than what most contemporary logicians would take as their subject matter.

Critical commonsensism. A doctrine defended by Charles S. **Peirce** largely in reaction to the Cartesian viewpoint (see **Cartesianism**). Whereas René **Descartes** proposed a method of inquiry beginning with universal doubt ("Begin by treating as absolutely false any belief that is in the least bit doubtful"), Peirce questioned the desirability and even possibility of such a procedure.

Peirce fully acknowledged that we may, in the course of an investigation, come to doubt what we began by believing; but, in such a case, we would have a positive, powerful reason for doubting. So he advised that we should not doubt in philosophy what we do not doubt in our hearts (CP 5.265). Common sense is nothing more, and nothing less, than what we do not doubt in our hearts—the whole stock of beliefs upon which we rely in countless contexts. But in order to distinguish his own commonsensism from traditional forms (especially the Scottish commonsensism of Thomas Reid and others), Peirce characterized his doctrine as critical, for it is imperative, on occasion, to examine critically even our most cherished beliefs. But such a critique can never be undertaken in the manner proposed by Descartes; it is rather an ongoing, piecemeal process in which we sift through our intellectual inheritance and commitments, relying on some parts of it in order to evaluate other parts. Peirce's critical commonsensism is an attempt to recognize both the need for criticism and the massive authority of our commonsensical beliefs.

Critique. In the most general sense, an evaluation. This term is frequently used in a narrower sense, one reflecting the usage of Karl Marx and subsequent writers concerned with emancipation in one form or another. (The influence on European semioticians of Marx and Sigmund Freud has been profound; Marxist and Freudian terminology are evident strands within the fabric of semiotic discourse.) So used, critique means a form of reflection whose proximate aim is critical consciousness (an awareness of truly what's what and who's who) and whose ultimate goal is liberation. Critical consciousness is to be understood in contrast to mystified consciousness. It is possible to be oppressed or exploited without being aware of this condition. This unawareness is ordinarily not simply a lack of consciousness but a *resistance to* facing what we perhaps dimly sense to be the case. Such unawareness, especially when resistance is a key or prominent feature, is called mystified (or naive) consciousness. The aim of critique is to challenge such unawareness in the name of liberation or emancipation. Today, however, thinkers like Michel **Foucault** and Jacques **Derrida** are so wedded to a **hermeneutic of suspicion** that the name of freedom, so drenched in the blood of innocent people, cannot be simply invoked or perhaps invoked at all.

Roland **Barthes** once confessed that, for him, semiology "started from a strictly emotional impulse." He felt that the study of signs "might stimulate social criticism," might provide more penetrating ways "of understanding (or of describing) how a society produces stereotypes, i.e., triumphs of artifice, which it then consumes as innate meanings, i.e., triumphs of Nature." Such a study was undertaken by him out of "an intolerance of this mixture of bad faith and good conscience which characterizes the general morality . . ." (*Barthes Reader*, 471). How is it possible to account for the fact that decent people either do or tolerate atrocious acts? If it is ordinarily not out of simple "natural" fears or hatreds but on the basis of myths (that is, *fabricated* fears, hatreds, desires, etc.), is it not crucial to understand the processes by which such myths are fabricated?

Cryptography, cryptology. Cryptography refers to secret writing and cryptology to the scientific study of such writing.

Culture. The totality of institutions and practices (including the forms of discourse) developed and sustained by some specific group of human beings. Ethnology, that branch of anthropology devoted to the study of culture, is a field from which a number of semioticians have come and, in turn, to which a number of others have been drawn. Claude Levi-Strauss's structural anthropology is perhaps the most famous endeavor to apply the insights of the linguist Ferdinand de **Saussure** to the investigation of culture.

D

DA. Discourse analysis.

Decentering of the subject. A dramatic shift away from the importance, prestige, or authority attached in **modernity** to the "**I**" or conscious, speaking, autonomous **subject:** This subject having moved from the center of the various discourses about human beings and things human (anthropology, psychology, linguistics, etc.) to the margins.

In the **modern** (or postmedieval) period, the individual in one guise or another (for example, that of individual consciousness as the arbiter of truth or that of the individual person as the bearer of rights) became more central than in previous epochs. The individual was treated primarily as an origin and only incidentally as an outcome— considered principally as the source from which thoughts, actions, feelings, etc. flowed and only rarely as something itself derivative. In **structuralist** and especially **poststructuralist** writings, the **subject** has been whisked off center stage. For example, language cannot be explained in terms of what images or ideas occur to the self; rather, the thoughts, actions, and even feelings of persons have to be interpreted in light of the linguistic, economic, cultural, etc. **systems** in which these persons are embedded. What was formerly at the center of the discussion—the self or "I"—has been pushed to the **margins,** and what was formerly on the margins—language and other systems—has become central.

Decoder. The **addressee** or receiver of a message, considered in its role of decoding or interpreting a message. The **addresser** or sender encodes a message, that is, transmits information by means of a code, while the decoder interprets this message in light of the same code. On this universally accepted model of communication, the possibility of communication depends upon a code shared by the participants in any communicative process. If two persons do not speak the same language, they might communicate by means of bodily gestures and facial expressions, but only because nodding the head up and down is taken by both parties to mean "Yes," nodding the head from side to side is interpreted by both as "No," etc.—that is, only because there is a code common to both.

Deconstruction, Deconstructionism. A contemporary intellectual movement especially in philosophy, literary theory and criticism concerned with (among other things) challenging the rigid or fixed hierarchies so central to Western thought and culture (for example, work/play; spirit/body; presence/absence; signified/signifier; speaking/writing).

To most of us, signs seem to be simply ways of representing objects, of bringing before consciousness something that might not otherwise be fully present to consciousness. Using words and gestures (that is, linguistic and other signs), I tell you about a storm that occurred while you were away. I was in the presence of the storm, while you were not. Thus you need to settle for a verbal representation. From such cases, it is natural to suppose that signs are insignificant whereas the realities to which they call our attention are what truly matter. Jacques **Derrida** challenges what he calls the metaphysics of presence, the view that, apart from signs, there are beings or events that might become fully present to consciousness. Within Western culture, the world apart from signs has traditionally been privileged over the world of signs. In response to George Berkeley's claim that *esse est percipi* ("To be is to be perceived"), Samuel Johnson kicked a stone and announced "I thereby refute him." The same impulse is often displayed in reaction to the deconstructionist claims that "There is nothing outside of the text" or "All **signifieds** are, in turn, themselves **signifiers.**" The import of these claims seems to be that there are no absolutely hard and fast objects, only unstable and fleeting signs, and this seems to be a gross violation of common sense. But, Johnson's act of kicking the stone was intended to show that the stone is something more than Berkeley's position could allegedly accommodate. For contemporary Johnsonian opponents of deconstructionism, there truly is a world apart from our signs: It is the world whose presence we directly encounter when we kick a stone or when something strikes us. For deconstructionists, there is also truly a world, but this world confronts us, first and last, as a text, an open-ended cluster of signs in which the play of meanings continuously undermines the possibility of fixing, once and for all, the meaning (and thus the reference) of any sign. The desire for a **transcendental signified** drives us to resist treating the world as a text: The desire to escape from the labyrinth of language is one with the desire to be in immediate contact with a transcendental signified. In the presence of such a signified, nothing more needs to be said; nothing more can be seen (or felt). But, at this point, defenders of deconstruction can appeal to our commonsensical intuitions. Does it not always turn out that there is more to say, a new interpretation or metaphor to be offered? And do not these sayings assist our seeings, do not these interpretations and metaphors sharpen and deepen our perceptions and sensibilities? Are not those who would arrest the play of signifiers presumptuous and, beyond this, tyrannical? For do they not assume the authority of policing thought and even of imprisoning signifiers within narrowly circumscribed cells? We cannot by a sheer act of will or intellectual sleight of hand make language or any other system of signs mean anything at all; it is rather that any utterance, text, or sign process always means more than, and even other than, what the utterer intended or could imagine. To trace the subtle and complex ways in which texts turn against and undermine themselves—to follow the ways texts deconstruct themselves—is the primary task of deconstructionist critics.

Deduction. A type of **inference** in which the **conclusion** is supposed to follow necessarily from the premises. For instance, if it is true that A is greater than B and that B is greater than C, then it is *necessarily* true that A is greater than C. In this example, A is greater than B and B is greater than C are the premises and A is greater than C is the conclusion. **Logic** studies the forms of inference.

Deep structure. A term encountered frequently in linguistics and not infrequently in **semiotics** (especially narrative analysis) and contrasted with surface structure. The deep structure is the underlying, largely hidden structure by which the surface structure of, say, a sentence or a narrative is generated. The concern to unearth deep structures has been a central preoccupation of linguistics as practiced by Noam Chomsky and his followers; it has also been a focal concern of narratologists (see narratology) such as Roland **Barthes** and A. J. **Greimas.** According to these theorists, it is as though one might X-ray a sentence or narrative and perceive the bare bones holding up the verbal or textual figure.

Defamiliarization. The term (along with "making strange") often used to translate the Russian word transliterated *Ostranenie,* the word used by the **Russian formalists** to identify the principal function of artworks. The principal function of poetry and presumably other artworks is to challenge our habitual modes of perception; it can only do so by a process of defamiliarization (or making strange).

Deictic. An adjective used by linguists and sometimes by **semioticians** to designate **signs** that refer directly to temporal, spatial, or personal aspects of the situation in which an utterance is made or a **discourse** takes place. Now/then, here/there, I/you, and this/that are deictic signs.

Denotation. See **connotation.**

Denotatum (plural *denotata*). Object, event, or being of whatever sort denoted by a word or expression; that to which a word or utterance refers. The terms denotatum and *sigificatum,* as they are used by Charles **Morris,** closely correspond to **reference** (*Bedeutung*) and sense or **meaning** (*Sinn*), respectively.

Derrida, Jacques (b. 1940). Contemporary French philosopher who has exerted a significant influence on literary theorists and critics as well as philosophers. He is a champion of **deconstruction.** This prolific author is often described as a poststructuralist (see **poststructuralism**). His books include *Speech and Phenomena and Other Essays on Husserl's Theory of Signs* (1967 [1973]), *Of Grammatology* (1967 [1976]), *Writing and Difference* (1967 [1978]),

Dissemination (1972 [1981]), *The Margins of Philosophy* (1972 [1982]). That he has written a 521-page book entitled *Post Card* (1980) reveals his playfulness and (in the often severe judgment of his critics) his excessive self-indulgence. One central concern of Derrida's deconstructionist critique is to undermine **binary oppositions**—to show how terms that appear to be mutually exclusive in fact depend on one another.

Descartes, René (1596–1650). An early **modern** philosopher who has exerted a profound and pervasive influence on later thought. In his attempt to offer a knock-down refutation of **skepticism,** he arrived at the position of "I think, therefore I am" (*Cogito, ergo sum*). Even on the strongest—and most far-fetched—hypothesis imaginable (that there is an evil spirit who is committed to deceiving me each and every moment of my life), I can be absolutely certain of at least one truth: I am (*sum*). For in order to be deceived, I must be. Therefore, the very possibility of doubt (doubt being a form of thought) insures the necessity of my own existence. So, if I think at all—even if my thinking is doubtful and erroneous in all other respects—I must *be* in some way. If there were no one to deceive, there would be no deception; if there is deception, there must be someone. Voila! I exist! What is even more important than this argument against skepticism is the starting point which Descartes bequeathed to later thought: individual consciousness as the arbiter of truth and the source of meaning. (See **decentering of the subject.**)

Charles S. **Peirce** suggested that "Descartes marks the period when Philosophy put off childish things and began to be a conceited young man. By the time the young man has grown to be an old man, he will have learned that traditions are precious treasures, while iconoclastic inventions are always cheap and often nasty" (CP 4.71).

Dewey, John (1859–1952). An American philosopher associated with the pragmatic movement. *Experience and Nature* (1925), *Logic: The Theory of Inquiry* (1938), and *Knowing and the Known* (1949) are especially important for assessing and appreciating Dewey's contribution to the study of signs and symbols.

Diachronic. From the Greek, *dia-*, through, across, and *chronos,* time. Dealing with phenomena (for example, the spelling of words or the rules of grammar) as these change over a period of time; roughly equivalent to historical or temporal.

Ferdinand de **Saussure** sharply distinguished the diachronic from the **synchronic** study of **language.** A diachronic investigation traces the development or evolution of language, whereas a synchronic inquiry examines language as a **system,** a network of relationships co-existing in the present. Saussure was reacting to the Neogrammarians of his own day, linguists who contended that the only valid approach to the study of language was a historical or diachronic approach. It is arguable that one extreme approach called forth the opposite extreme, for an exclusive concern with the history of language was displaced by a systematic denial of this history's relevance for an understanding of language. In order to make his case persuasive, Saussure was forced to draw another sharp distinction. Language (*langue*) should not be confused with **speech** or **discourse** (*parole*). Language is, according to Saussure, a self-contained whole (1916 [1966], 9) and thus an appropriate object of synchronic study. Thus, not only is Saussure's model of the sign **dyadic** (since it is a correlation of two items—an acoustic image and its corresponding concept, for example, the sound "dog" and the idea this sound calls to mind), his orientation toward the study of linguistic and other signs is based on several **dichotomies.** The two just mentioned—diachronic/synchronic and *langue/parole* (language/speech)—are at the center of Saussure's project.

Diacritical. Adjective meaning distinctive or distinguishable. In order for anything to function as a sign, it needs to be distinctive or distinguishable from the other items used also as signs. Because he focused considerable attention on how signs are generated by their differences—by the way or ways they can be distinguished from other signs in the same **system** (for example, the same **language**)—Ferdinand de **Saussure**'s conception of **sign** is sometimes called diacritical. See also **articulation, binary opposition.**

Diagram. A type of sign in which the **iconic** function is the predominant sign function but also in which the symbolic and indexical functions are clearly present. See **index, symbol.**

If a coach diagrams a play on a blackboard, he is constructing a sign that in some important respects resembles its object; thus it is iconic. But the diagram also relies on **conventions** and indices. There is the convention of using X's to designate players on one team and O's players on the other team. In addition, the X's and O's have an indexical function. A coach draws three X's and says, "Szykula, this is you; Alan, that's you; and Vinnie, this is you—so this is where the ball will be."

Charles S. **Peirce** devoted attention to diagrams, noting explicitly that they combine iconic, symbolic, and indexical functions. "A diagram is," in his words, "a

87

representamen which is predominantly an icon of relations and is aided to be so by conventions. Indices are also more or less used" in diagrams (CP 4.418).

Dialectic. In the most general sense, a process involving opposites (for example, one might say that history is a dialectic of spontaneity and constraint); more narrowly, a process resulting in a synthesis or reconciliation of opposing forces or factors.

Dialogism. A doctrine or orientation based upon dialogue. Dialogue, a semiotic process of mutual give and take, is often used as a model to explain or illuminate phenomena not ordinarily considered in reference to this process. For example, **experience** has been conceived as a process of dialogue—a give and take between the self and others. Such a view was defended by the American pragmatists Charles S. **Peirce** and John **Dewey.** So understood, experience is not primarily subjective, but essentially intersubjective: Its locus is neither inside nor outside the self, but between selves. Martin Buber's category of the between was designed to show a way out of the impasses arrived at by thinking exclusively in terms of inner and outer, subjective and objective, private and public. So, too, has **thought** been construed as dialogue. In several of Plato's dialogues, we find the characterization of thinking as the soul conversing with itself; and Peirce never tired of insisting that all of our thought takes the form of a dialogue. He went so far as to claim that "[s]uccessful research . . . is conversation with nature . . ." (CP 6.568). Dialogism is a term often used to describe Mikhail **Bakhtin**'s conception of language. See also **conversation, tuism.**

Dialogue. A type of discourse characterized by a give and take among several participants; a literary genre modeled on conversation (for example, Plato's dialogues). Martin Buber has examined the nature and forms of dialogue, paying especially close attention to dialogue as an existential encounter between I and Thou; Mikhail **Bakhtin** and Hans-Georg Gadamer have also devoted considerable attention to this process of give and take.

Dicent. A term introduced by Charles S. **Peirce** to designate a specific type of **sign** or **sign function;** namely, one corresponding roughly to a statement. This sign is part of a triad or **trichotomy: rheme, dicent,** and **argument.** Peirce derives this trichotomy by considering the sign's relation to its **interpretant.** His classification of signs on this basis yielded what is called, in traditional logic, concepts, statements, and arguments. That is, rheme, dicent, and argument more or less correspond to concepts, statements, and arguments, respectively.

Dichotomy. A twofold division or distinction, especially one between mutually exclusive things. While a **trichotomy** cuts things in threes, a dichotomy cuts them in two. See also **dualism.**

Dicisign. A term used by Charles S. **Peirce** as a synonym for **dicent,** a sign roughly corresponding to a statement in the context of its utterance.

Dictionary vs. **encyclopedia.** Two contrasting ways of explaining the meaning or content of **sememes** (the most basic units of **meaning** within a semiotic **system,** ordinarily understood as a **language**). The model of the dictionary is based on the assumption that there are ultimate sememes in terms of which all other units of meaning (all other sememes) are derivable. The Porphyrian tree (named after the late-classical Greek philosopher Porphyry or Porphyrius, c. 232–c. 303) is an example of such a "dictionary." All substances can be differentiated into immaterial and material (spiritual and corporeal substances); in turn, all bodies (or material substances) can be differentiated into animate or inanimate (living or nonliving); animate substances can, in their turn, be divided into animal and vegetal, etc. In contrast, the model of the encyclopedia is offered to show the way the content of any sememe whatsoever is established in and through its connections with virtually all other units of meaning. Encyclopedias have to be continually updated, for what counts as a fact at any given time often is demoted in light of later research. But encyclopedias include information about what has been taken to be a fact at some time or by some group. This information is taken as part and parcel of what a term means. A full account of "Sun" as a sememe would require noting that it was taken by certain cultures to be a golden chariot blazing across the sky and that today it is conceived as a star or largely gaseous mass in process of continuous explosions. While a dictionary constructed along the lines required by Porphyry's conception of definition would be a series of dichotomous branchings, an encyclopedia would be a vast, complex net in which one could move from any given node to any other, although it may demand the most circuitous of routes.

Différance. A word coined by Jacques **Derrida** as part of his critique of **phonocentrism** and of the metaphysics of **presence.** It involves a pun, for he is playing on two senses of *differ:* to differ and to defer (postpone or put off). In addition, this word itself is supposed to show the dependence of speech upon writing, for the difference to a French speaker between *difference* and *differance* is no difference at all. That is, the difference is discernible to the eye but not to the ear.

Difference. Otherness; opposition (see **binary opposition**). In both **structuralism** and **poststructuralism,** much is made of difference. It is used to explain how the most basic units in language are generated; the rhetoric of difference (and otherness) is also used to make evident the subtle yet powerful ways in which important differences are concealed and even repressed. "We perceive differences," A. J. Greimas notes, "and thanks to that perception, the world 'takes shape' in front of us, and for our purposes" (1966, 19).

Definiendum. Latin word referring to a word or expression being defined, in contrast to the *definiens* (the definition or expression offered as such). In defining "hammer" as "a tool designed for pounding and pulling nails and similar objects," "hammer" is the *definiendum* and "a tool, etc." the *definiens.*

Ding an sich. German expression meaning "thing in itself" and ordinarily contrasted with appearance or **phenomena** (the thing as it appears to us) or with **representation** (the thing as it is represented by us). The **modern** German philosopher Immanuel Kant sharply distinguished things in themselves from things as they appear to us, maintaining that our knowledge is limited to appearances. Charles S. **Peirce,** one of the **contemporary** co-founders of **semiotics,** rejected the notion of an unknowable *Ding an sich.*

Discourse. A term sometimes used to translate *parole* (more usually rendered "speech"). Ferdinand de **Saussure** separated **language** (*langue*), conceived as a self-contained system of formal differences, from speech (*parole*), the actual utterances of individual speakers. He did so for the purpose of making language the formal object of linguistics and he thought that the study of language should focus on language, not speech or discourse. While language conveys to many the notion of **system** (a resource upon which speakers can draw), discourse and speech suggest process, engagement, and entanglement—the struggles in which historically situated agents engage. The expression "*dominant* discourse" is often used to mean the discourse that has dominated and, as part of this, excluded the possibility of other discourses (the discourse of others, for example, women or people of color).

Discourse analysis (DA). The **analysis** of **language** (*langue*) and/or **speech** (*parole*) (depending on the theoretical commitments of the particular author) above the level of the sentence. The investigation of linguists has tended to focus on the sentence and on the units (for example, **phonemes** and **sememes**) and rules used to generate sentences. For this reason, Roland **Barthes** and other semioticians have undertaken a "second linguistics," "a linguistics of discourse," to exhibit these units and rules of discourse. Traditional linguistics is not to be faulted, only supplemented: In Barthes's own metaphor, having described the flower, the botanist is not obliged to describe the bouquet. But others might feel and, in fact, have felt the need to describe the ways the flowers have been arranged into bouquets (that is, discourses). Narrative analysis (NA) is perhaps the most highly developed part of discourse analysis. But NA is only one form of DA.

Discourse analysis should not be confused with **conversation analysis** (CA). DA is almost always undertaken in accord with structuralist principles and is thus a largely formal, deductive approach. In contrast, CA is an empirical, inductive approach, devoted to examining recordings and, more recently, videotapes of actual conversations.

Discursive practice. A term designed and used to highlight the fact that the various **discourses** in which we engage (for example, philosophy, literary criticism, political commentary) are themselves practices and, moreover, are practices that intersect with other nondiscursive practices. What and how we read and write or hear and say, bear upon how we and others make a living and, in countless other ways, participate in the various practices by which needs are satisfied, desires generated, and so on, and thus by which society itself is reproduced. See also **praxis.**

Displacement. A Freudian term designating the process, or result, of redirecting an emotion or impulse from its original object to a more acceptable one. When a child who is angry at a friend expresses hostility toward a sibling, the anger is displaced. Displacement has been invoked along with **condensation** by psychoanalytically oriented semioticians and even others to illuminate the way language works.

Dissemination. A term used by Roland **Barthes** and especially Jacques **Derrida** to suggest the essential openness and productivity of a text. According to such literary semiologists as Barthes and Jacques Derrida, the function of a text is not representative, but productive: It is not a mirror being held up to nature, history, the psyche, or anything else, but rather a mechanism productive of meaning. The text is not a finished product but an openended process in which the reader has the obligation to assume the role of co-author. To assume this role would, in effect, mean rewriting the text; and to rewrite the text "would consist only in disseminating it, in dispersing it within the field of infinite difference" (Barthes, 1974, 5).

Distinction. The process of marking differences; the result of such a process. It is helpful to distinguish, perhaps even to separate, the process of distinguishing from that of separating two or more things. It is one thing to distinguish two things, quite another to separate them and thereby imply that they are separable (that is, that they can exist apart from one another). While Ferdinand de **Saussure** claimed that **language** and speech are separable, Roland **Barthes** has maintained that they are merely distinguishable: "Language flowers out into discourse; discourse flows back into language; they persist one above the other like children topping each other's fists on a baseball bat" (*Barthes Reader*, 471).

Double Articulation. See articulation.

Dream. A phenomenon that, according to Sigmund Freud, Jacques **Lacan,** and other thinkers, should be treated like a text. A dream, no less than a novel or play, is above all an invitation to interpretation. Lacan and others have combined the resources of psychoanalytic and semiotic theory in their approach to interpreting dreams.

Dualism. A twofold distinction. Like dichotomy, *dualism* suggests a sharply drawn distinction, often between mutually exclusive or completely different things. For example, René **Descartes**'s conception of the human person is often described as dualistic, a being composed of two fundamentally different kinds of things or substances (an immaterial mind and a physical body).

According to Charles S. **Peirce,** "[w]e naturally make all our distinctions too absolute" (CP 7.438). The result is often a dualistic outlook. Peirce suggested that dualism "in its broadest legitimate meaning" is "the philosophy which performs analyses with an axe, leaving as the ultimate elements, unrelated chunks of being" (CP 7.570). In structuralist linguistics and the semiological tradition modeled on such linguistics, this is arguably the case with the dualistic way in which Ferdinand de **Saussure** and his followers have distinguished **language** (*langue*) and speech (*parole*). Necessary distinctions should not be elevated to absolute separations. See also **synechism.**

Dyad. Pair; sequence, process, or anything else having two parts, sides, or dimensions.

Dyadic. Two-termed. The dynamic duo of Batman and Robin is a *dyadic* combo. (There is a technical mathematical sense of this term, but it is almost never the sense in which *dyadic* is used in semiotics.)

E

Eco, Umberto (b. 1932). Contemporary Italian semiotician, medievalist, and novelist. His work in **semiotics** ranges from highly technical and theoretical questions to analyses of comics such as *Superman* and *Krazy Kat*. His characteristic playfulness is revealed in one of his definitions of semiotics: This discipline "is concerned with everything that can be *taken* as a sign"—anything that can be substituted for something else. "This something else does not necessarily have to exist. . . . Thus, *semiotics is in principle the discipline studying everything which can be used in order to lie*" (1976: 7). In an interview in 1986, Eco confessed that "[e]very single thing I've done comes down to the same thing: a stubborn effort to understand the mechanisms by which we give meaning to the world around us" (Sullivan 1986, 46; quoted in Noth 1990, 326).

Economy, principle of. The principle according to which the maximum of achievement is attained through the minimum of effort (or output). See also **abridgement**.

Écriture. Common French noun for "writing," "script." When this French word is left untranslated in an

English text, it is likely that the term is being used in one or more senses established by a **contemporary** French author. In one sense, *ecriture* refers to writing as an intransitive activity, a conception proposed by Roland **Barthes.** See **writing.** In another sense, it means writing as *différance,* a position propounded by Jacques **Derrida.** See **arche-writing.** In still another sense, it means writing as an activity in which sexual differences can be discerned. *Ecriture feminine* (sometimes translated as "writing as a woman") is the form of writing in which the specific and irreducible **gender** of a female writer or speaker shapes both the form and the content of her utterances.

Écrivain. A term used by Roland **Barthes** and others to designate what is often translated as "author"; the producer of texts for whom the verb "to write" is intransitive. In this sense, **writing** calls the reader's attention to the activity of writing itself rather than to something else. An author (*ecrivain*) in this respect differs from a writer (*scripteur, ecrivant*), for "writers" subordinate writing to something other than itself.

Écrivant. See *Écrivain.*

Ego. The Latin word for "I," often used as a psychoanalytic term denoting a specific part of the human psyche: that part defined by the role of mediating between either the id and reality or the id and the superego.

Sigmund Freud's psychoanalytic theory has influenced such thinkers as Jacques **Lacan,** Julia **Kristeva,** and Luce **Irigaray.** In fact, Freud is important for both the contributions his own writings make to an understanding of signs (for example, his work on the interpretation of dreams) and the influence of these writings on others. This demands a basic familiarity with some of the key terms in Freudian and, more generally, psychoanalytic discourse.

Emic/etic. Adjectives coined by Kenneth L. Pike to designate two different approaches to the study of such things as **language** or **culture,** an emic approach being one that is specifically adapted to one language or culture, while an etic approach is one of general applicability.

In semiotic studies, signs may be investigated etically or emically. A **typology** of the signs applicable to a number of systems would be etic, while a description of the functions of the signs peculiar to one particular system would be emic.

Empiricism. The doctrine that all knowledge is based on **experience** or observation. In opposition to the claim that the human mind possesses innate ideas, John **Locke** and other empiricists argued that, at birth, the mind is a tabula rasa (blank slate), the only ideas it possesses being those it acquires in the course of experience. Some empiricists (for example, Charles S. **Peirce**), however, have argued that even if some of our ideas are innate and thus not derived from experience, they can only be justified by appeals to experience. For them, the justification (rather than the origin) of our ideas is the decisive issue.

Sometimes *empiricism* is used in a negative sense to designate the naive orientation of those who contend that the facts speak for themselves and, hence, the task of interpretation is avoidable. In opposition to this orientation, there are those who contend not only that the facts cry out for interpretation but also that what counts as a fact changes (see **episteme, paradigm shift**). For them, facts are the products of complex, evolving processes of intervention (for example, the experiments of physicists or the observations of anthropologists in the field). See also **rationalism.**

Encoder. Addresser or **utterer;** transmitter of a **message** by means of a **code.** See also **decoder.**

Encyclopedia vs. **dictionary.** See **dictionary** vs. **encyclopedia.**

Engendering of subjectivity. The process by which a human organism, as a result of being initiated into various systems of **representation,** becomes a **subject,** a split being (conscious/unconscious) with a sexual or gendered identity. The expression involves a pun, since it plays upon two senses of *engendering* (the process of bringing something into being and the process of acquiring a **gender**). The term *subject* itself is often used in a way that plays upon its etymology, for it commonly refers to a being who has undergone a process of subjection; that is, a process in which our libidinal drives are subjected to societal inhibitions.

Enlightenment, The. A specific epoch in Western history extending from the late seventeenth to the late eighteenth centuries (often identified as the Age of Reason); a set of ideals (most prominently, reason, freedom, progress, and nature) championed during the Age of Reason and supposed by some to possess universal or transhistorical validity. Two slogans capturing the sensibility of the Enlightenment are in fact two injunctions: Horace's *Sapere aude!* ("Dare to know!" or, more loosely, "Dare to think for oneself!"), quoted by Immanuel Kant at the outset of his essay "What Is Enlightenment?" and Voltaire's *Erasez l'infame* ("Crush the infamy!" or "Destroy the institution!").

The postmodern sensibility is, to a significant degree, a radical critique of such Enlightenment ideals as reason, freedom, progress, and nature. In the name of reason, many irrational beliefs have been defended; in the name of freedom, countless acts of tyranny have been undertaken; in the name of progress, the natural environment has been defiled and whole cultures annihilated. Hence, abstract appeals to these allegedly universal ideals need to be viewed with suspicion; detailed attention must be paid to what is actually being done, by whom, to whom, and for whom.

Enthymeme. An **argument** in which a part (either one of its premises or its **conclusion**) is unstated.

Énoncé vs. *enonciation.* French terms used to draw a distinction between what is uttered (the *enonce*) and the process or act of utterance (*enonciation*). In accord with a precedent set by the linguist Emile **Benveniste,** *enonciation* is often used to designate the act by which the utterer assumes a position within language. The assumption of such a position inevitably involves taking part in a complex, historical process. Upon any participant in such a process, the force of various forms of oppression will be exerted; but, then, so will the possibilities for various kinds of liberation be available. These particular features of enunciation have been a central concern of feminists.

Episteme. A Greek word for knowledge. A term introduced by Michel Foucault and widely used to denote the underlying, largely hidden grounds on which a statement or claim counts as knowledge during a particular period of human history. In the Middle Ages, theology counted as the highest form of knowledge ("the queen of the sciences"), while today it does not in most circles count as knowledge at all. The reason is that there has been a shift from one *episteme* to another (see *coupure epistemologique* and **paradigm shift**). What counted as *scientia* (or knowledge) in the Middle Ages is quite different from what counts as knowledge today. The grounds have shifted.

In *The Order of Things* (*Les Mots et les Choses*) (1966), Michel Foucault examined three different periods (the Renaissance, the Enlightenment, and the period from the nineteenth century to modern structuralism) in light of his notion of *episteme*. At this time, he claimed that "[i]n any given culture and at any given time, there is always only one *episteme* that defines the conditions of possibility of all knowledge" (1966, 168). Eventually he denied that his notion of episteme is a "basic" or "fundamental" category for the interpretation of history and thus ceased to use this notion. But texts and ideas have a life of their own, so one frequently encounters the notion of *episteme* in writings of thinkers who have been influenced, directly or indirectly, by Foucault.

Epistemological. Pertaining to knowledge.

Epistemology. The study of knowledge; more fully, the investigation of the origin, nature, limits, justification, and forms of knowledge. Many semioticians believe that the formal and systematic study of **signs** has the capacity to transform this traditional branch of philosophy.

Epistemology has been a focal concern of Western philosophers, especially in the **modern** period. In many quarters of **contemporary** thought, however, there has been rejection of epistemology-centered philosophy.

Erasure. A term used by **deconstructionists** such as Jacques **Derrida** to signify the inescapability of relying on terms at once inadequate but necessary. Derrida borrowed from Martin Heidegger this practice of writing *sous rature* (under erasure). The very word *sign* is so deeply part of a tradition in which the **transcendental signified** occupies the highest possible place that anytime we use the word we necessarily suggest the signified (that which is what it is in itself, apart from all representation). But, in order to discredit the notion of a transcendental signified, Derrida has no option but to use the very language that in some respects reinforces the very view he is attacking. Such a practice indicates the necessity of situating oneself within a framework in order to destroy it.

Erklarung. German word for explanation, often used in contrast to *Verstehen* (understanding). It is frequently supposed that natural phenomena (for example, an eclipse) call for explanation, whereas cultural artifacts (texts, buildings, systems of law) call for understanding. It is further supposed that *Erklarung* and *Verstehen* are irreducibly different processes. See also **Geisteswissenschaften.**

Ethics of terminology. A set of rules or guidelines for how to devise and use terms, especially technical terms in a scientific discipline or a discipline striving to transform itself into a science. In order to facilitate the transformation of philosophy into a science, Charles S. **Peirce** developed an ethics of terminology.

Exegesis. An explanation or interpretation of a text. The processes by which texts are explained or interpreted have been the central concern of thinkers in the **hermeneutic** tradition, for instance, Friedrich Schleiermacher (1768–1834), Wilhelm Dilthey (1833–1911), Hans-Georg Gadamer (b. 1900), and Parl Ricoeur (b. 1913). These processes are obviously also of interest to semioticians.

Experience. A term often taken to mean what occurs *inside* a person or organism; a term redefined by Charles S. **Peirce** and the other American pragmatists to mean what goes on *between* the self and the world. In the first sense, the expression "subjective experience" is pleonastic or redundant. It would be analogous to saying "a deceptive liar." But the conception of experience as intrinsically subjective or private is what many semioticians, especially ones rooted in the Peircean tradition, reject. For them, experience has the form of a dialogue: It is the ongoing give and take between a conscious, living being and its world. As a consequence of this give and take, human organisms acquire the capacity for self-communication (that is, thought) and for self-concealment. There thus arises a very real sense of an "inner" life. But this life should be seen for what it is: a derivative and complementary process. What is primary and complemented here is the dialogue between self and other. In this sense, experience is what the German word *Erlebnis* suggests—the ongoing, transformative process of *living through* various, overlapping situations and, in addition, the cumulative product of this process.

John Deely offers an explicitly semiotic description of human experience: "[t]he semiotic point of view is the perspective that results from the sustained attempt to live reflectively with and follow out the consequences of one simple realization: The whole of our experience, from its most primitive origins in sensation to its most refined achievements of understanding, is a network or web of sign relations" (1990, 13). See also **empiricism, intersubjectivity.**

Expression vs. **content.** A set of terms used by the linguist Louis Hjelmslev to rename what Ferdinand de **Saussure** called the **signifier** and signified, respectively. For Saussure, a **sign** is a two-sided entity: One side is called the signifier, the other is called the **signified.** Hjelmslev developed what has been called a stratified or multilevel dyadic model of the sign (1943, 58; also Noth 1990, 67). This model is dauntingly complex, as are many of Hjelmslev's other notions. But at its center is the dyadic (or two-termed) relation between the expression form and the content form. This is the nucleus of the sign in Hjelmslev's sense. It shows the influence of Saussure and, in turn, has influenced such contemporary semioticians as Roland **Barthes** and Umberto **Eco.**

Expressive. The function of communication whenever the process is directed toward the sender or addresser of a message.

F

Fallacy. An invalid argument; more generally, a mistaken viewpoint or erroneous statement.

Fallibilism. The doctrine that any of our claims about reality are liable to be erroneous or susceptible to error. This doctrine should not be confused with **skepticism** in its extreme sense (that is, in the sense that skepticism amounts to a denial of the possibility knowing reality). For the fallibilist, absolute certainty is an unattainable ideal for human investigators; nonetheless, we more or less securely know countless things. Charles S. **Peirce,** one of the founders of contemporary **semiotics,** strongly advocated this doctrine.

Family resemblance. A notion designed by Ludwig **Wittgenstein** to show that the generality of a word can be explained without supposing that there is a single essence possessed by everything that can be properly designated by that word. In his *Philosophical Investigations*, Wittgenstein invites his reader to consider "the proceedings we call 'games.' I mean board-games, card-games, ball-games, Olympic games, and so on. What is common to them all?—Don't say: 'There *must* be something common, or they would not be called 'games'—but *look and see* whether there is anything common to all' " (#66). When we do look, what we see is "a complicated network of similarities overlapping and criss-crossing: sometimes overall similarities, sometimes similarities of detail." Wittgenstein thought that there was "no better expression to characterise these similarities than 'family resemblances' " (#67). The word "game" does not have one essential meaning: It is meaningfully used in various ways and these varieties of **usage** have family resemblances. This means that there is not one property or set of properties found in all the activities to which the word *game* properly applies. Here he is characteristically calling our attention to the complexity of ordinary language.

Fashion. An area of semiotic inquiry opened up, in a systematic way, by Roland **Barthes**'s *The Fashion System* (1967 [1983]). Just as our buildings are designed to do more than shelter us (see **architecture**), our clothes are fashioned to do more than clothe us (see **polyfunctional**). They are one of the ways we make statements about ourselves. The exploration of these "statements" and related matters falls to semiotics, especially insofar as there might be a **code** or set of codes by which such statements are made.

Firstness. See Categories, Peircean.

Form of life (*Lebensform*). An expression used by Ludwig **Wittgenstein** and his followers to designate the totality of institutions, practices, and discourses in which a **language-game** (another central Wittgensteinian notion) alone makes sense. The language-game of bidding at an auction only makes sense against a backdrop of intersecting institutions, practices, and discourses; apart from this backdrop, the shouts of the bidders would be little more than sound and fury, signifying nothing.

The notion of *Lebensform* was designed by Wittgenstein to illuminate that language is not an abstract system but a set of practices embedded in a way (or form) of life. The way to understand language is not by abstracting it from the **context** of human action and experience, but by seeing that to share a language people must share a form of life.

Function. A task or role to perform; the act or manner of acting by which this task or role is performed; the relationship between two variables.

Roman **Jakobson** identified six possible functions in our communicative exchanges. When such an exchange is oriented toward (or directed to) the **addresser** or sender of a message, it serves an **emotive** function; when it is oriented toward the **addressee,** a **conative** function; when oriented toward the **context,** a referential function; toward the **contact** or **channel** of communication, a **phatic** function; toward the **codes** making possible the exchange, a **metalingual** (metalinguistic or metasemiotic function); toward the **message** itself, a **poetic** or **aesthetic** function.

The term *function* also occupies a central place in **narratology** (see **actant**).

G

Geisteswissenschaften. A German word designating the human sciences as distinct from *Naturwissenschaften* (the natural sciences). It has been and, to a large extent, still is customary to distinguish the human sciences as studies aiming at understanding (*Verstehen*) and the natural sciences as investigations aiming at explanation (*Erklarung*). The human sciences (*Geisteswissenschaften*) roughly correspond to what, in Anglo-American discourse, are called the social sciences. But since the context in which the human sciences have been pursued has been in some respects significantly different from that in which our own social sciences have been pursued, there are important differences. Not the least is that in Continental Europe the human sciences have not been modeled on the natural sciences, whereas in Great Britain and to an even greater extent in the United States they have.

Gender/sex. Gender is ordinarily taken to be a socially constructed form of identity, whereas sex is a biologically inherited set of traits. See also **engendering of subjectivity.**

General. A term often used by Charles S. **Peirce** as a noun to designate a property or regularity open to an indefinite number of instantiations or exemplifications. A **habit** is an example of a general in this sense; the same habit (say, pig-headedness or generosity) can be present in a countless number of people. Not only are generals open to unlimited instantiations, but many of them are themselves the source of unlimited events or acts. Peirce held that some generals are real, a position he called scholastic realism.

Gestalt. A whole that is perceived as such and that is not reducible to the mere sum of its parts.

Glotto-, glutto-. From the Greek word for tongue. Related to language or, more narrowly, to spoken language.

Glottocentrism. Any approach in **semiotics** that takes **language,** especially spoken language, to be the central or most important **system** of **signs.** Often this approach not only makes language the principal object of study but also studies all other systems of signs in terms of language (that is, in terms of the categories and distinctions derived from an investigation of language). Ferdinand de **Saussure**'s *semiologie* is glottocentric. Language is, for him, not only the most complex and universal system of expression but also the most representative and illuminating. It is for this reason that Saussure put forth linguistics (or the science of language) as "the master-pattern for all branches of semiology," even though language is only one particular semiological system among countless others (68).

Glottogenesis. The origin or evolution of a **system** of phonemic signs. It is now generally thought that glottogenesis began only about fifty thousand years ago. See also **semiogenesis.**

Grammar. Set of rules governing the formation and combination of the basic units in a semiotic system.

Grammatology. A term introduced by Jacques **Derrida** to designate his own theory of writing in general. It is, however, somewhat misleading to use "theory" in this context (even though Derrida himself does), since one of his objectives is to show that a theory or science of writing is impossible. Grammatology is intended to replace the general theory of signs and ultimately to undermine the metaphysics of presence. Traditionally, we have assumed that speaking is primary and writing derivative: Graphic signs are based on auditory signs; we have also assumed that we can come, as it were, face to face with reality.

Greimas, Algirdas Julien (b. 1917). An influential **contemporary** semiotician and narratologist. His writings include *Structural Semantics* (1966 [1983]), *Du sens* (1970), *Pour une theorie du discours poetique* (1972), and *On Meaning* (1987).

Ground. A term used by Charles S. **Peirce** to denote the respect or respects in which anything is equipped or designed to function as a **sign vehicle** (to stand for something other than itself). Not all the properties of a sign vehicle are relevant to its functioning as such. Whether a stop sign is made of wood or metal is inconsequential; however, whether it is octagonal or triangular, or whether it is colored red or green, is crucial. Whatever functions as a stop sign does so by virtue of a specific set of properties. These properties of the sign, taken together, are called its ground, since they provide the basis that enables an entity or event to serve as a sign vehicle.

Some contemporary interpreters of Peirce (most notably T. L. Short) have made a persuasive case for the view that the general notion of ground came to be replaced by a specific classification of sign functions—the classification of signs considered in reference to their objects. According to this classification, some things are equipped to be sign vehicles because of their resemblance to their objects, in which case they function as **icons;** other things are equipped to be sign vehicles because of an actual, physical connection with their objects, in which case they function as **indexes;** still other things are so because of a habitual connection between themselves and their objects, in which case they function as **symbols.** To classify a sign vehicle as iconic, indexical, or symbolic, then, indicates the respect in which it is equipped or designed to stand for its object. Hence, this specific classification can be seen as replacing the general notion of ground.

H

Habit. A disposition to act in certain ways in certain circumstances, especially when the agent is animated or guided by certain motives (see, for example, CP 5.480). For Charles S. **Peirce,** the **meaning** of **signs** is best understood in terms of the habits they generate, sustain, and modify. When I say that a knife is sharp, I mean that it has the capacity to cut through various things. My dispositions to use instruments for cutting combined with my motive to avoid injury are, pragmatically, what sharpness *means*. See also **belief, general, pragmatism**.

Haecceitas, **hecceity.** "Thisness"; having the status or properties of being an individual existent, in contrast to a general nature. *Haecceitas* was a term used by the **medieval** philosopher John Duns Scotus to designate the principle of individuation (the principle by which a common nature such as humanity is individuated in countless individuals). This term was adopted by Charles S. **Peirce** and used for the same purpose, to identify the principle of individuation (see, for example, CP 1.341; 1.405). See also **general,** *hic et nunc,* **individual**.

Hermaneutic, hermeneutics. This term (derived from the name of Hermes, the Greek god who served as herald and messenger for the other gods) is often used in a wide sense to mean the art or theory of interpretation, though its original meaning was the interpretation of sacred scripture. There is a tradition of reflection on the nature and forms of interpretation. This tradition includes such nineteenth-century thinkers as Friedrich Schleiermacher and Wilhelm Dilthey and such twentieth-century ones as Martin Heidegger, Hans-Georg Gadamer, and Paul Ricoeur. It is both a rich tradition and of direct relevance to some of the most central concerns of **semiotics**.

"According to its original definition, hermeneutics is," in the words of Gadamer, "the art of clarifying and mediating by our own effort of interpretation what is said [or written] by persons we encounter in tradition [that is, at some remove, historical or cultural, from ourselves]" (1976, 98).

Hermeneutics of suspicion. An expression introduced by Paul Ricoeur to designate an approach to the interpretation of a text or discourse in which the principal concern is to uncover what is *not* said rather than to recover the meaning of what has been said. This approach strives to bring to the surface what characteristically remains hidden in, but vital—often even central—to the text or discourse. Karl Marx and Sigmund Freud are often considered masters of the hermeneutic of suspicion, for Marx is bent on unmasking ideological distortions and Freud on exposing unconscious motives. Friedrich Nietzsche is also widely recognized as a thinker uncannily adept at revealing what is going on "behind the scenes."

Heterocriticism. Criticism directed at a person by someone else, by someone other than (hetero-) the person being evaluated or criticized; thus, the opposite of self-criticism (or **autocriticism;** also **critique.**)

Charles S. **Peirce** defined the **normative sciences** as those philosophical disciplines concerned with providing a general theory of deliberative conduct (of action open to ever more refined forms of criticism, revision, and control). He maintained that "[i]f conduct is to be thoroughly deliberate, the ideal must be a habit of feeling which has grown up under the influence of a course of self-criticism and hetero-criticism . . ." (CP 1.574). The ultimate wellspring of our actions—our feelings about what is fine or noble, admirable or lovely, in itself and thus what is most worthy of concrete embodiment—should be subjected to both autocriticism and heterocriticism.

Heuristic. Serving as an aid to learning, discovery, or inquiry. When Charles S. **Peirce** describes his universal **categories** as having a heuristic function, he means that they are instruments or tools to be used in the investigation of any topic whatsoever.

Hic et nunc. Latin for "here and now." The hereness and nowness of things was taken by the **medieval** thinker John Duns Scotus and, much later, by Charles S. **Peirce** to account for their "thisness" or individuality (the fact that a thing is this, rather than that, is determined by its being here rather than there and its occurring now rather than then). In other words, hereness and nowness are the marks of individuality. An individual is something actually existing here and now or in a series of spatiotemporal locations. According to Peirce, the mode of being exemplified by an individual existent is very different from the mode exemplified by a general nature (for example, humanity). See also **haecceitas, general, individual, reality**.

Homo loquens. The language-using or speaking animal. This has been one of the various ways the human species has been named and, in effect, defined. The most common name is, of course, homo sapiens. But, in addition to *Homo loquens*, alternative designations include *homo faber* or *homo habilis* (the user and maker of tools); *homo prometheus* (the user of fire); *homo ridens* (the laughing animal); *homo ludens* (the playful animal); and *homo politicus* (the political animal). Ernst **Cassirer** proposed *animal symbolicum*.

Humanism. A term often used in a very broad sense to denote the affirmation of the value and dignity of human beings; in a more restricted sense, one referring to a cultural and intellectual movement, beginning in the Renaissance (if not even earlier) and animated by a specific image of human beings. **Consciousness,** autonomy (understood principally in the negative sense of

111

freedom from the constraints of tradition and the will of tyrants), individuality, and control over nature are among the most salient features of this image. See also **anti-humanism.**

Hypostatic abstraction. A form of **abstraction** identified and emphasized by Charles S. **Peirce.** He distinguished between two types of abstraction, hypostatic and **prescissive** (see, for example, CP 4.235). By *prescissive* abstraction, he meant pretty much what is today simply called *abstraction;* by *hypostatic* abstraction, he meant the process by which a predicated quality or formal operation is converted into an ens rationis (being of reason)—into, as it were, an entity in its own right. An example of hypostatic abstraction is to take the proposition "The dress is white" and make of the predicated quality (white) a subject of which other qualities might be predicated ("Its whiteness was brilliant"). Something analogous or similar might be done to formal operations: Some operation might itself become something upon which another operation is performed. The operation of conjoining two elements might, for example, be the subject of an inversion: Having conjoined (A + B), we might derive (B + A). Hypostatic abstraction enables us to make a subject of a predicate or to operate upon what is itself an operation. While "economic actor" is an example of a prescissive abstraction (for it is derived by selecting, for purposes of a focused inquiry, certain features of multidimensional agents and ignoring countless other features), "poverty" appears to be the result of a hypostatic abstraction (a subject derived by converting a predicated quality—"He is poor"—into a term of which other things might be predicated or said—"Poverty is soul-destroying").

The theory of sign generation and sign interpretation itself depends on abstraction. Peirce himself suggested that "The wonderful operation of hypostatic abstraction . . . furnishes us the means of turning predicates from being signs that we think or think *through,* into being subjects thought of. We thus think of the thought-sign itself, making it the object of another thought-sign" (CP 4.549; cf. CP 2.227). Signs are best described as neither inputs nor outputs, but as throughputs, for they put one thing through to another. They forge connections between or among things that would otherwise be separate or unrelated. Thus they often, perhaps characteristically, perform their function by effacing themselves, by calling attention to other things rather than to themselves. Insofar as I stare at the letters of a word as objects in their own right, I become absorbed in them; such absorption can be so complete that the shapes to which I am attending have ceased to be signs, precisely because I am attending *to* them rather than *through* them to another. They are objects, foci upon which my attention is fixed—not signs, vehicles by which my attention is conveyed. Even so, signs as signs can, in some manner and measure, be made the objects of attention and thus of investigation. For Peirce, the manner in which this is accomplished depends, above all, on hypostatic abstraction.

Hypothesis. A guess or conjecture put forth to explain something puzzling (see **phenomenon**). Charles S. **Peirce** sometimes used this term as a synonym for **abduction.** He maintained that inquiry involves the interplay among the three forms of **inference.** Hypothesis or abduction is, in a way, at the center of this interplay, for the principal function of **deduction** is to derive consequences from hypotheses and the main task of **induction** is to test hypotheses in terms of these consequences. Peircean semioticians often contend that when we read a text we are engaging in just such a process of **inquiry**.

I

"**I.**" The first person singular pronoun, often used in semiotic writings as a noun, designating the **subject.** One reason "I" is used in this way is to underscore the insight of the linguist Emil **Benveniste** that it is only in and through language that humans constitute themselves as *subjects.* The subjectivity intended here is defined not by privacy but by reflexivity, not by being invisible to others but by being able to speak about and to refer to oneself. See also **cogito, engendering of subjectivity.**

Icon. A term used by Charles S. **Peirce** to designate a specific type of **sign** or **sign function** in which the **sign vehicle** represents its **object** by virtue of a resemblance or similarity. A map is an example of an icon, since it represents a region or terrain by means of a discernible *isomorphism:* the configurations on a sheet of paper resemble the configurations of a region (the curved line resembles a meandering river, a grid of lines a network of streets, etc.).

Peirce's definition of icon is part of an intricate classification of signs. Here it is sufficient to note that icon is part of a triad including **index** and **symbol.** Peirce considered this *triad* (or **trichotomy**) to be "the most fundamental division of signs" (CP 2.275); it has certainly been one of the most influential of all Peirce's semiotic doctrines.

The basis for this *trichotomy* is the relationship between the sign and its object. (The bases for the two other trichotomies are, on the one hand, the nature of the sign itself and, on the other, the relationship of the sign to its **interpretant**.) If a sign is connected with its object by virtue of a resemblance to that object, it is an icon. If it is related to its object by virtue of some physical or actual connection (for example, the weathervane being moved by the wind and thereby pointing out the wind's direction), it is an index (or indexical sign). If a sign is connected with its object by virtue of some habit or disposition, either innate or acquired, it is a symbol.

The recognition of icons in Peirce's sense seems to threaten the importance attached to **arbitrariness** by Ferdinand de **Saussure** and thinkers influenced by him. Even Umberto **Eco,** a thinker who draws heavily upon Peirce's doctrine of signs, feels compelled to offer a critique of iconism (1976, 191ff).

Iconicity. Having the status or properties of an **icon;** fulfilling the **function** or playing the role of an icon (a sign which represents its object by virtue of a resemblance to that object).

Id. Latin for "it," often used as a psychoanalytic term designating the vast, impersonal region of the psyche underlying both the **ego** (or "**I**") and the *superego* (or "over-I"). It is the locus of our drives and the source of the *libido.*

Both Karl Marx and Sigmund Freud have exerted a wide and deep influence on semioticians, especially in Europe. Terms drawn from Marxist discourses make up one important strand in the fabric of semiotic writings, while those drawn from Freudian discourses make up another. One of the most basic terms in Freud's psychoanalytic vocabulary is, of course, the id.

115

Ideological superstructure. A term inspired by Karl Marx's writings and used to designate the **discursive practices** (theology, philosophy, literature, etc.) generated and sustained by an economic basis. The distinguishable disciplines and discursive practices both grow out of and feed into the economic base; but for Marx and his followers, the economic base is primary and the ideological superstructure is derivative. The use of the expression *discursive practices* is intended to highlight the fact that even our theoretical pursuits are historically evolved and evolving practices. Such pursuits depend upon the allocation of limited resources; and apart from the desires or intentions of their practitioners, they serve in some manner and measure the powers responsible for allocating these resources.

Ideology. In Marxist discourse, a term ordinarily meaning "false consciousness"; more generally, a system of ideas in the service of some group. In this more general sense, we could speak (as Marx himself often did) of a revolutionary ideology; that is, a system of ideas serving those who would wrest power from the hands of the status quo). In addition to conceiving ideology as a system of ideas bearing upon the maintenance, augmentation, usurpation, etc. of power, it is also helpful to conceive all discourse whatsoever as ideological or involving an ideological dimension. All uses of signs, in one way or another, bear upon the possession of power; since they do, all signs exhibit an ideological dimension. The writings of Michel Foucault and feminist authors such as Luce **Irigaray** explore the omnipresent yet subtle presence of this dimension.

Idiolect. A unique or idiosyncratic language (*langue*) or form of discourse (*parole*).

Illocution; illocutionary act or force. Illocutionary act, an utterance that entails the execution of an action, ordinarily an institutionally or socially recognized form of action (in the very act of uttering the proper words in the appropriate circumstances—"I baptize you Peter Carlo"—the minister executes the rite of baptism); illocutionary force, the dimension or aspect of an utterance amounting to any action. In everyday life, many of our utterances ordinarily amount to actions—for example, making promises or hurling insults, offering praise or giving directions. The effect of the utterance on the hearer or addressee is called the **perlocutionary force.** So, when a speaker or addresser says "I am tired" and the hearer or addressee, rightly, comprehends this to mean "Let's go home," the hearer might feel irritation or even resentment. This feeling would be the perlocutionary force of the utterance.

Imaginary order or **register.** A term used by Jacques **Lacan** to designate one of three orders (or domains) of the human **subject**'s experience. The other two are the **symbolic** and the **real** orders. The imaginary order (often simply called the imaginary) is pre-Oedipal, whereas the introduction into the symbolic order and the Oedipal conflict are different aspects of the same process. The imaginary is the order of our experience dominated by identification and duality; it not only precedes the Oedipal conflict but it coexists alongside the symbolic order even after the eruption of this conflict.

Immediate knowledge. Often used as a synonym for **intuitive knowledge;** knowledge unmediated by any factors (for example, signs). In the colloquial sense, an intuition is a hunch or intimation. Due to the influence of Charles S. **Peirce** and others, this term often means something quite different in semiotic discourse; it signifies an instantaneous, immediate, and infallible grasp of some object or event.

An example of what is (allegedly) intuitive or immediate knowledge would be Robinson Crusoe's direct perception of Friday. Before directly perceiving the other inhabitant of the island on which he was marooned, Robinson Crusoe possessed only discursive or mediated knowledge of there being someone else living there. From fresh footprints he inferred that he was not alone. What Peirce and others insist is that perception as a form of knowledge is different not in kind, but only in degree, from all other forms of human knowledge. Even our direct perceptions of objects and events are instances of an interpretation-laden and inference-generated process of knowing. See also **abduction.**

Index. A usage established by Charles S. **Peirce** and widely adopted by contemporary semioticians to denote a specific type of **sign** or **sign function** in which the **sign vehicle** represents its **object** by virtue of an actual or physical connection. For example, the weathervane is an index since it indicates the direction of the wind by virtue of an actual connection between the wind and itself.

According to Peirce, signs may be related to their objects in three different ways: on the basis of a resemblance or similarity (such signs being **icons**); on the basis of an actual or physical connection (indexes); or on that of a habit, either innate or acquired (**symbols**). Indexes (also called indexical signs and, occasionally, indices) are those signs in which the **sign vehicle** is actually or physically connected with its object.

Individual. A term often used in contrast to the **subject;** a term also used by Charles S. **Peirce** in a sense closely linked to the etymology of the word *individual* (that which is indivisible or that which cannot be decomposed into anything simpler or smaller). Let us consider both of these senses in some detail.

To conceive human beings as individuals is one thing and as subjects quite another. The dominant image of human beings inherited from Western **humanism** is that of individuals defined as conscious, unified, and autonomous beings. For postmodernists such as Michel Foucault, Jacques **Lacan,** and Jacques **Derrida,** each aspect of this image needs to be contested or at least severely qualified. The very image of ourselves as individuals needs to be replaced by an understanding of our status as subjects. Specifically, this means that we need to shift the emphasis from consciousness to the unconscious, from unity to division, and from individual autonomy to cultural overdetermination. The subject is not only a split or divided being (conscious/unconscious) but also one in which consciousness plays a largely superficial and ineffectual role. The scope of our freedom is extremely limited, if not entirely illusory, since our actions, thoughts, and even desires are so thoroughly and relentlessly conditioned by cultural forces.

In contrast to **generals,** individuals in Peirce's sense are existents or actualities whose mode of being amounts to crowding out a place for themselves in the here and now. He sometimes referred to individuals in this sense as "logical atoms" since they are entities thought to be incapable of being resolved into anything smaller or simpler. He denied the existence of such atoms, contending that the only beings with which we have any acquaintance are ones which are not absolutely individual (that is, thoroughly anti-general). Consequently, absolute individuality is, for Peirce, an ideal limit approximated by actualities or existents compulsively experienced here and now.

Induction. A probable inference. In an inductive argument, the premises or evidence render a conclusion likely or probable, whereas in a deductive argument the premises are put forth as though they render the conclusion necessarily true. Charles S. **Peirce** stressed that, in our inquiries, the three forms of inference—induction, **deduction,** and **abduction**—work together. Abduction is the process by which hypotheses are formed, deduction the process by which the necessary consequences or entailments of hypotheses are established, and induction the process by which they are tested.

Not infrequently, induction is used in a loose and, in the judgment of logicians, incorrect sense to mean the process of going from particular truths to general or even universal truths. Parallel to this sense of induction, deduction is—again, loosely—the process of going from general or universal to particular truths.

Inference. The process by which one statement is derived from one or more other statements; the form in accord with which such a process occurs. If you know that A is older than B and, in turn, that B is older than C, you can infer that A is older than C. The process of deriving "A is older than C" from the two other statements is an inference; it is based on a general form or pattern found in countless other inferences.

Infelicitous, infelicity. Terms used by J. L. **Austin** to designate the way in which an **utterance,** other than a **constative** (an utterance of which it makes sense to ask whether it is true or false), is inappropriate, untoward, or inept. If I say that Thomas Jefferson was the first president of the United States, my utterance is false (for such an utterance is a constative); but, on March 28, 1989, if I promise to meet you on March 26, my utterance is not false but infelicitous. So, when the utterance of a promise, vow, etc. is poorly or even wrongly executed, it is a mistake to say that is "false"; rather we should say that it is "infelicitous."

Inquiry/conversation. Inquiry, a process undertaken for the sake of discovering the truth; conversation, an exchange undertaken for its own sake and refusing to acknowledge any "extraconversational constraints." Charles S. **Peirce** defined inquiry in a very broad sense as any process in which **doubt** is overcome and **belief** secured or fixed. He and others have supposed that inquiries or investigations are undertaken for the discovery of previously unknown truths and that philosophy is—or should aspire to be—a form of inquiry. Richard Rorty has recently proposed to replace inquiry (or investigation) with conversation. The point of human discourse is not to copy reality (to hold a mirror up to nature or history) but to cope in ever more creative ways with the actual circumstances into which we have been thrown. See also **conversation/inquiry, dissemination.**

Intentionality. A term used to denote the fact that **consciousness** in all of its manifestations is depicted as being always a consciousness or awareness *of* something. This feature or property of consciousness has been stressed by phenomenologists.

Interpretant. A term used by Charles S. **Peirce** to refer to one of the three essential parts of a **sign** or of a process of **semiosis.** According to him, a sign is irreducibly triadic, its components being the sign (or **sign vehicle**) itself, the **object,** and the interpretant. The interpretant should not be confused with the interpreter:

The interpretant is that in which a sign *as such* results, whereas the interpreter is a personal agent who takes part in and presumably exerts control over a process of interpretation. The interpretant is not any result generated by a sign. Something functioning as a sign might produce effects unrelated to itself as a sign; for example, a fire indicating the presence of the survivors of an airplane crash might set a forest ablaze. The forest fire would be an incidental result and thus not an interpretant of the sign calling for help (or indicating the whereabouts of the survivors).

Interpreter. A person who engages in a process of interpretation, of making sense out of some **text, discourse,** or other semiotic phenomenon. The interpreter should not be confused with what Charles S. **Peirce** calls the **interpretant.** In *The Problem of Christianity*, Josiah Royce formulates a theory of interpretation in which the role and status of the interpreter is stressed. While in this work he explicitly acknowledges his debt to Peirce's theory of signs, he also goes beyond this theory, developing a part of semiotics Peirce himself did not explore in much detail.

Peirce sometimes uses **utterer** and interpreter to designate, respectively, the **sender** and **receiver** of a message.

Intersemiotic. What takes place between two different sign systems. In contrast, the **intrasemiotic** pertains to or occurs in the *same* sign system.

Intersubjectivity. The condition of two or more distinct subjects or persons being related in some way to each other. If the **subjective** refers to an inner or private domain, and if the **objective** refers to an outer or public sphere, the intersubjective designates, first and foremost, what goes on *between* two persons (or among three or more persons). Obviously most forms of communication are intersubjective. Since thought might best be viewed as the self engaged in **dialogue** with itself, we should refrain from classifying *all* communication as intersubjective. Frequently, we assume that something is either subjective or objective: It takes place either *inside* the self (moreover, a self in isolation from others) or *outside* the self. The concept of intersubjectivity helps us to see that most (if not all) human experience and action goes on *between* the self and others. Signs might be defined as the media for this ongoing, transformative dialogue between self and others.

Some semioticians (for example, Charles S. **Peirce** and Mikhail **Bakhtin**) go so far as to affirm the primacy of intersubjectivity. See also **intertextuality.**

Intertextuality. A term introduced by Julia **Kristeva** and widely adopted by literary theorists to designate the complex ways in which a given text is related to other texts. Just as there is no **sign** apart from other signs, there are no texts apart from other texts. In Kristeva's words, "every text is constructed as a mosaic of other texts, every text is an absorbtion and transformation of other texts. The notion of intertextuality comes to replace that of **intersubjectivity**" (Kristeva 1969, 146).

The term *intertext* might mean either a text that draws upon other texts or a text drawn upon by another text. Sometimes this word also means the relationship between two texts or among several texts.

Intrasemiotic. Pertaining to or occurring in the same semiotic system (or system of signs). **Intersemiotic,** in contrast, refers to the relationship between two distinct sign systems. When one saxophonist responds to another in an improvisational piece, there is an intrasemiotic exchange, for both are operating within the sign system of music. However, when a dancer translates these musical improvisations into improvisational movements, there is an intersemiotic exchange.

Intuition, intuitive knowledge. A synonym for **immediate knowledge.** Charles S. **Peirce** used *intuition* in a technical sense to mean a cognition determined not by any other cognition but solely by an object outside consciousness. The **conclusion** of an **argument** is obviously a cognition determined by other cognitions, whereas the perception of a table is apparently a cognition determined solely by an object outside consciousness (the table itself). For this reason, perception has been viewed as an intuition, an instance of immediate (that is, unmediated) knowledge. In denying that there are intuitions in this sense—in insisting that all our cognitions are mediated by signs of various sorts—Peirce opened the door to a thoroughly semiotic account of human cognition or knowledge.

Irigaray, Luce (b. 1933). A **contemporary** French feminist critic and theorist whose deconstructive readings of Western philosophy and psychoanalytic theory have exerted a wide influence in both the United States and Europe.

Irredicible, irreducibility. Irreducibility, the property or status of not being reducible or dissolvable without loss into anything simpler; irreducible, not dissolvable without loss into any simpler. At the center of Charles S. **Peirce**'s understanding of **signs** is the claim that signs are irreducibly triadic or three-termed (see *triad*). Compare these two triadic relationships, A moves from B to C and A gives B to C. According to Peirce, the first of these can be reduced, without loss, to a pair of dyadic relationships—A departed from B and A arrived at C. In contrast, the act of giving is not the accidental conjunction of two disparate acts—A discards B and B comes into the possession of C. In the act of giving, three terms (the giver, the gift, and the recipient) are indissolvably linked together; that is, giving is irreducibly triadic.

Iteration, iterability. Iteration, the process or activity by which something (say, a **sign**) is replicated or reproduced; iterability, the capacity for repetition or reiteration; to be able to be repeated or produced again and again. This is commonly assumed to be an essential feature of signs. Charles S. **Peirce** is explicit on this point: "The mode of being of a **representamen** [or, more simply, a sign] is such that it is capable of repetition" (CP 5.138).

J

Jakobson, Roman (1896–1982). A contemporary linguist whose work represents an important synthesis of the Saussurean and Peircean traditions of semiotic research. "The subject matter of semiotics is," according to Jakobson, "the communication of any messages whatsoever, whereas the field of linguistics is confined to the communication of vernal messages. Hence, of the two sciences of man, the latter has a narrower scope, yet, on the other hand, any human communication of non-verbal messages presupposes a circuit of vernal messages, without a reverse implication" (Quoted in Noth 1990, 75).

Jouissance. A French word meaning ectasy or bliss,

often used to describe the experience of sexual orgasm. Roland Barthes used this word to identify a specific kind of text and, related to this, a specific experience of reading. See also **bliss, texts of.**

K

Kristeva, Julia (b. 1941). A contemporary semiotician whose work draws heavily upon her psychoanalytic background. According to Kristeva, investigators of signs should strive to make semiotics more than "an empirical science aspiring to the modeling of signifying practices" by means of logical formulas. "At every instant of its production, semiotics thinks of its object, its instrument and the relation between them." So conceived and undertaken, it is "an open form of research, a constant critique that turns back on itself and offers its own autocritique" (Quoted in Noth 1990, 322).

L

Lacan, Jacques (1901–1981). Contemporary French psychoanalyst and theorist who has exerted a significant influence on semiotics today. His contribution is often described as a far-reaching re-interpretation of psychoanalysis from a structuralist perspective. In particular, his conception of the three orders or registers of human experience—the **Imaginary,** the **Symbolic,** and the **Real**—have been appropriated by contemporary semioticians.

Lack. A term used by Jacques **Lacan** to designate a felt, animating absence or deprivation. His usage carries echoes of Hegel (1770–1831), a philosopher who highlighted "the portentous power of the negative." This power is manifest in desire: a felt *lack,* an urgent sense of *not* having something or being someone other than who one actually is, exerts an inescapable and often tyrannical power over human beings. This lack underlies all striving. Desire implies the absence of satisfaction and, in turn, satisfaction the fulfilling of desire. But can desire be fulfilled, can it be fully filled such that a sense of lack never recurs? The total cessation of desire is found only in death. Life is, in contrast, the continuous renewal of desire, the ceaseless return of felt lacks—though often in different forms and at different levels than previous desires and satisfactions. Our felt lacks are not simply physiological, but inherently symbolic. The food, drink, clothes, and persons we desire are the objects of not purely organic drives but a culturally overdetermined subjectivity. Lacan's psychoanalytic theory focuses on lack in this sense, highlighting its "portentous power" and its inevitable frustration. While desire ineluctably drives us, satisfaction continuously escapes us. These are, in truth, simply two ways of saying the same thing.

Langer, Susanne (1895–1985). American educator and philosopher whose contribution to semiotics in the United States include *Philosophy in a New Key: A Study in the Symbolism of Reason, Rite, and Art* (1942), *Feeling and Form* (1953), *Mind: An Essay on Human Feeling* (volume I [1967], volume II [1972], and volume III [1982]). Central to her study of symbolism is a sharp distinction between discursive and presentational (or nondiscursive) forms of symbolization. Language is a discursive form, art a nondiscursive or presentational form. In response to the way Langer draws and applies this distinction, one is perhaps tempted to recall that "[w]e naturally make all our distinctions too absolute" (CP 7.438). The study of symbols "has arisen in the fields that the great advance of learning has left fallow. Perhaps it holds the seed[s] of a new intellectual harvest, to be reaped in the next season of human understanding" (1942, 33). Like Charles S. **Peirce** and Ferdinand de **Saussure** before her, Langer envisioned a comprehensive study of human symbols holding the promise of deepening our self-understanding.

Language. The term often used by semioticians and others in a very general sense to mean any system of signs. It is also frequently used in a narrower sense to designate a system of **verbal** signs, taking *verbal* here to include both spoken (or auditory) and written signs. Third, *language* is used in a still narrower sense by some linguists (for instance, Ferdinand de **Saussure** and Leonard Bloomfield) and others to mean a system of auditory signs. "Language and writing are," in Saussure's words, "two distinct systems of signs; the second exists for the sole purpose of representing the first" (1916 [1966], 23).

The **function** of language as significant speech was taken, in the dominant traditions in Western thought during the ancient and medieval periods, to be the communication of ideas, intentions, feelings, etc. This suggests another definition: Language is an instrument or means of communication. But if we think of tools or instruments in the ordinary sense of these words, there's something misleading about this definition. For while we can pick up and put down a hammer or saw, we cannot divest ourselves of our languages: They are so deeply a part of ourselves that to be stripped entirely of our languages would be like being deprived completely of our bodies. What would be left? Often we seem to imagine ourselves as disembodied spirits and our thoughts as extralinguistic and even extrasemiotic entities; but it is not clear whether either a human being or human thinking is possible apart from some form of concrete embodiment. In the case of persons, that form is of course what is ordinarily called the body—the flesh-and-blood organism born of woman and man; in the case of thought, it is some system of signs. Hence, language in the broadest sense noted above is as much an instrument of thought as it is one of communication.

This observation brings up the important question of whether there can be thought apart from language taken in the narrower senses (specifically, as a system of verbal signs or, even more narrowly, a system of spoken signs). At one extreme, there are those who affirm this possibility; at the other, those who deny it. For Charles **Peirce,** all thought is in signs though not necessarily in words. For John **Dewey,** "If language is identified with speech, there is undoubtedly thought without speech. But if 'language' is used to signify all kinds of signs and symbols, then assuredly there is no thought without language . . ." (1931 [1960], 90). For these two pragmatists (see **pragmatism**), there can be extralinguistic but not extrasemiotic thought—thought apart from verbal signs but not thought apart from some species of signs and symbols. But both also realized that, for a species of animal that has acquired the use of linguistic or verbal signs, thought involves an intricate and inevitable interplay between linguistic and nonlinguistic signs. How these animals use nonlinguistic signs is influenced or conditioned by their language, narrowly understood, and even in those instances where thinking is conducted in nonlinguistic signs—for instance, mathematicians (who think primarily in diagrammatic signs), painters (who think principally in visual signs), or musicians (in purely acoustical signs)—linguistic signs often play a supplemental role. This position does justice to several equally important features of human thought: the importance (perhaps even paramount importance) of spoken and written language; the variety of irreducibly different sign systems used by human beings; and the likelihood, if not inevitability, of interplay among these sign systems in any actual process of human thinking (see **thought**).

In conclusion, it would be helpful to recall Roman **Jakobson**'s observation that "the image of language as a uniform and monolithic system is oversimplified. Language is a system of systems, an overall code which includes various subcodes" (1985, 30).

Language vs. (speech or discourse). See *Langue* vs. *Parole.*

Language game. An expression introduced into philosophy by Ludwig **Wittgenstein** and designed to serve several purposes, above all, that of underscoring two important features of human languages: (1) the conventional and contextual character of our linguistic practices and (2) the irreducible variety of tasks made possible by language. Part of Wittgenstein's aim was to replace the view of language as a **nomenclature** (a set of names) with a more accurate and nuanced view.

Langue vs. *Parole.* French terms customarily translated, respectively, as language and speech (or discourse).

In his *Course in General Linguistics,* Ferdinand de **Saussure** separated *langue* from *parole.* Saussure was concerned with reorienting linguistics (the study of language) from a historical or **diachronic** study to a systematic or **synchronic** investigation. He rejected the possibility that linguistics could, let alone should, try to combine diachronic and synchronic forms of investigation. The pivot around which this reorientation of linguistics turned was the separation of language (*langue*) from speech or discourse (*parole*).

This **binary opposition** has deeply informed **structuralism** and **semiotics.** Indeed, structuralism is largely a generalization of Saussure's approach to the study of language: The way the author of the *Course in General Linguistics* proposed to investigate *langue* can be adapted to the study of culture (for example, Claude Levi-Strauss), or mind (Jean Piaget), or the unconscious (for instance, Jacques **Lacan**).

Latent vs. **manifest content.** Latent content, the hidden content or meaning of a message or other configuration of signs (for example, a **dream**); manifest content, the surface meaning. One dreams of being chased by lions and tigers and bears. The dream is *manifestly* or apparently about lions and tigers and bears: This is its manifest content. But its latent content might be the anxiety felt by the most successful stockbroker in a firm feels as her associates begin to approximate her performance. Today *subtext* is often used as at least roughly equivalent to latent content.

Lebenswelt. German word for Life-world; the world of everyday experience. The *Lebenswelt* is the matrix from which all action and reflection emerge and the **context** in which all of our engagements and theorizing must ultimately be situated. In this context, *life* should not be construed primarily in a biological sense. *Lebenswelt* refers not so much to the world of living things as to that of our distinctively human lives. The term was used by Edmund

Husserl (1859–1938) in late manuscripts not published during his lifetime and, then, was adopted as a key word in Maurice Merleau-Ponty's (1908–1961) critical appropriation of Husserlian **phenomenology.**

Legisign. A term coined by Charles S. **Peirce** to designate a specific type of **sign** or **sign function,** specifically, one in which a law, regularity, or **general** serves as a **sign vehicle.** A word is an example of a legisign.

Throughout his life, Peirce tried to construct a comprehensive and systematic classification of signs. A threefold consideration is at the center of what is perhaps his most successful attempt at such a classification. This consideration is based on the very nature of a sign, as defined by Peirce: anything (thus, something in itself) standing for some other (called its **object**) and giving rise to an **interpretant.** Accordingly, signs might be considered in themselves, or in relationship to their object, or finally in relationship to their interpretants. These three consideration yield three **trichotomies:** a sign considered in itself might be a quality and thus a **qualisign,** an individual thing or event, thus a **sinsign,** or a law, hence a legisign; a sign considered in relation to its object might be an **icon** or **index** or **symbol;** a sign considered in relation to its interpretant is a **rheme** or **dicent** or **argument.** See also **type** vs. **token.**

Lexical, lexicon. Lexical, pertaining to or found in a dictionary; lexicon, dictionary. The lexical meanings of a word are those meanings recorded in a dictionary.

Linerarity. A term used by Ferdinand de **Saussure** to designate one of the two most basic properties or features of **signifiers:** the property of being part of a chain or sequence in which the presence of one signifier necessitates the displacement of previous ones. Saussure identified **arbitrariness** and linearity as the "two primordial characteristics" of the linguistic sign (67).

Linguistic turn. One of the most important developments in twentieth-century Anglo-American philosophy, in which language became both an object of investigation and the principal means by which philosophical disputes are to be solved or, in at least some cases, dissolved. Professional philosophy in the United States and Great Britain turned away from some of its traditional concerns and turned toward language as its principal concern. G. E. Moore, Bertrand Russell, A. J. Ayer, Ludwig **Wittgenstein,** J. L. **Austin,** and John Wisdom are among the more important names associated with reorienting philosophy to a preoccupation with language. Early in this development, the dream of constructing an ideal language exerted a powerful influence, especially among **logical positivists;** eventually, a deep respect (often bordering on reverence) for ordinary language replaced the various attempts to construct an ideal language.

Lisible. A French word meaning legible or readable but often translated "readerly." Roland **Barthes** used this term to identify a particular kind of **text,** one in which the **reader** is called upon to do nothing more than consume a pregiven meaning. See also **writerly.**

Literal vs. **metaphorical** (or **figurative**) **usage.** Literal usage, a way of using language characterized by adherence to the primary lexical meanings of words; metaphorical usage, a use of language in which words or expressions are stretched beyond their recognized senses (see **metaphor**). When used in a *literal* way, words and expressions are employed in more or less strict conformity with their established meanings. Presumably the word "lamb" in "Mary had a little lamb" is being used in a literal

133

way to designate a specific kind of animal. Language is used metaphorically (metaphor means transfer, a carrying from one place to another) when there is a transference of a term from its "**proper**" sphere. When a congregation refers in prayer to Christ as "the lamb of the world," the word "lamb" does not refer to an animal but to a person: The term is being used in a *metaphorical* way.

There is an immense and still-growing literature on metaphor. The concern of some writers on this topic is to challenge what is taken by them to be the dominant traditional view of metaphor as merely an embellishment. They argue that many metaphors have cognitive significance: They are indispensable instruments by which we know some aspect of reality. They are not stylistic flourishes, but cognitive tools—not ornaments, but truly instruments for knowing. Another concern has been to challenge the hierarchy implied in the distinction between literal and metaphorical uses of language. Traditionally, the literal has been defined as the proper use of language, one in accord with established usage or meaning; in contrast, the metaphorical has been linked with impropriety or violation. A metaphor violates the established rules of literal meaning. While it does so deliberately and, moreover, often heightens effect and even deepens understanding, metaphor is an intrinsically derivative or parasitic use of language, as the metaphorical use of language would be impossible apart from the literal use. Recently there has emerged, especially among deconstructionists, a pronounced tendency to call into question any and all rigidly fixed hierarchies in which one term is privileged and the other denigrated. The hierarchy of literal (proper) vs. metaphorical (improper) use is often assumed to be an instance of a fixed hierarchy.

Literariness. The set of traits, conventions, and devices that distinguish the literary use of language from other uses. The identification of these traits, conventions, and devices was a central preoccupation of the Russian formalists (see **Russian formalism**).

Locke, John (1632–1714). Modern British philosopher whose *Essay on Human Understanding* (1690) provides a defense of **empiricism,** the doctrine that all ideas and thus all knowledge are derived from **experience.** In the final chapter of his *Essay* ("Of the Division of the Sciences"), Locke (apparently influenced by the ancient Stoics) divides the field of human inquiry into three regions: "All that can fall within the compass of human understanding" itself falls under three headings: *phusike* or natural philosophy (the "knowledge of things, as they are in their own proper beings, then constitution, properties, and operations"); *praktike* (the "skill of right[ly] applying our own powers and actions, for the attainment of things good and useful"); and *semeiotike* or the doctrine of signs. The "business" of this doctrine "is to consider the nature of signs" as they are used by the mind either for the understanding of things or the conveying of knowledge to others.

Locutionary force. The inherent force or meaning of a statement in contrast to both its effect upon a hearer and also its status or **function** as an action. J. L. **Austin** distinguished the locutionary force of utterances from their illocutionary and perlocutionary force. If I say "You can trust me—I'll be there," the locutionary force of this utterance is nothing more than what these words mean. In most contexts, such an utterance would constitute a promise: In saying these words, I am in effect doing something—namely, making a promise. This would be the illocutionary force of my utterance. Finally, the effect of this utterance on my hearer—say, the engendering of trust or confidence in my being where you agreed to meet me—is the perlocutionary force of my words.

Logic. The study of the types or forms of **inference.** The systematic analysis and evaluation of the forms of inference can be traced as far back as Aristotle. In this long history there is much of direct relevance to **semiotics.**

Charles S. **Peirce,** one of the co-founders (along with Ferdinand de **Saussure**) of contemporary semiotics, conceived logic as a **normative science** divided into three parts: **speculative grammar, critic,** and **speculative rhetoric** or **methodeutic.** What today is called logic corresponds to what Peirce called critic.

Considered as a normative science, the objective of logic is to show how we, as inquirers, ought to conduct ourselves in any context of **inquiry** (or truth-seeking). If we are animated by the desire to discover the truth (or, put another way, to arrive at the most reliable and comprehensive account of some topic), certain ways of acting will facilitate the realization or, at least, approximation of this goal, while other ways will frustrate inquiry. The task of the logician is to identify the forms of conduct that facilitate inquiry. Here *conduct* is to be understood in a very broad sense, covering all the ways we conduct ourselves, with the implication that we can exert some measure of control over our conduct. The forms of inference are, in this sense, forms of conduct, for they are at bottom the ways we conduct ourselves as thinkers (the way we carry on the business of thinking or investigating).

A normative approach to human conduct thus concerns itself with attaining a fuller awareness of what we have done or are doing and, on the basis of this awareness, a finer evaluation of our achievements and our undertakings. Such an evaluation is, in turn, oriented toward acquiring fuller control over ourselves and our conduct. In short, self-consciousness is ordered to self-criticism and, in turn, self-criticism is ordered to self-control. Just as mathematics evolves out of more rudimentary practices or activities—counting, adding, subtracting, etc.—so too logic evolves out of more rudimentary activities, the most rudimentary of which is that of "putting two and two together," of drawing inferences of one sort or another. And just as mathematics progresses by virtue of its ability to devise symbols far removed from the activities out of which it originated, so too logic progresses by virtue of this same ability. Devising such symbols involves abstracting from any and all content; and such **abstraction** allows the logician no less than the mathematician to consider procedures in a purely formal manner. But such procedures, no matter how abstractly and formally conceived and studied, are procedures—ways human inquirers propose to undertake or carry on the business of thought. And, as such, they are criticizable in light of the norms and ideals of inquiry. Part of what motivates the formalization of these procedures, especially in the case of logic, is the felt need for a canon of criticism, the means by which missteps in inference or proof might be detected and thus avoided.

Logical positivism. An influential philosophical movement during the first half of this century, originating in the 1920s around a group of philosophers, scientists, and intellectuals in Vienna known as the Vienna Circle. At the heart of logical positivism (also, but less frequently, called logical empiricism) is the principle of **verifiability:** The only meaningful statements are those that are, in principle, open to verification. On the basis of this criterion of cognitive meaning, much of traditional philosophy and theology was dismissed as nonsense. According to the logical positivists, the views of most of their philosophical predecessors were not false; their failure was more fundamental—they were meaningless.

Logocentrism. The orientation of those who privilege *logos,* identity, self-same form and presence over *dynamus* (force or power), **difference,** and **traces.** Logocentrism is the allegedly dominant bias or fixation of Western thought and, more generally, culture. It is the ineluctable drive for a transcendent moment in which all differences are eliminated, all flux is regulated, and all meanings are fixed. To make *logos* (itself the very image of harmony and commensuration) the center entails seeing conflict and incommensurability as eradicable defects of human discourse. For deconstructionists such as Jacques Derrida, however, conflict and incommensurability are ineliminable features of all discourses. See also **deconstructionism, transcendental signified.**

Logos. A Greek word having various meanings, the most prominent of which are word, **argument, discourse, language, reason.** To get some sense of this term's importance, it is helpful to recall the opening sentence of the Gospel of John: "In the beginning was the Word [Logos] and the Word was made flesh." This usage clearly indicates that, in the West, Logos has been one of the names of God. This word has also been used to identify the capacity that allegedly distinguishes human beings from all other animals.

M

Manifest content. What a message or other configuration of signs (for example, a **dream**) manifestly or (on the surface) straightforwardly conveys. The *manifest* content is often construed as something superficial, that is, floating on the surface, while the **latent content** is something hidden or buried beneath the surface. It is customary to conceive what is latent as more important or real than what is manifest, though deconstructionists such as Jacques Derrida have challenged the tendency to privilege of the hidden and the deep over the accessible and the surface.

Margin, margins. A commonly encountered **metaphor** in **contemporary** writings used to **thematize** what has been unduly neglected or devalued. The metaphor of marginality and periphery has become a central **trope** in deconstructionist and postmodernist writings. It is inevitable in any discourse that some topics occupy center stage and others seem to be inconsequential or even irrelevant. But it is illuminating to consider *what* and, even more significantly, *who* gets marginalized in a text or tradition of writing, for marginalization both reflects and sustains the relations of power within a culture or institution (see **ideology**). Thus deconstructionists advocate "reading from the margins," paying attention to apparently inconsequential connections or accidental associations, for the purpose of showing how texts function as instruments of suppression.

Marked Signifier. A term indicating that a **signifier**

or **sign vehicle** is marked—qualified or modified in some way. The linguist and semiotician Roman **Jakobson** developed a theory of markedness. For example, the verbal signifier "cat" in the singular is unmarked and in the plural (cats) is marked by the addition of "s."

The way *markedness* tends to be used today concerns the **ideological** dimension of human **communication** or **discourse;** that is, the dimension bearing on relationships of power within a culture or some narrower context (for example, a church or business). Take the expression "female judge" or "Hispanic legislator." Here the signifier or sign vehicle "judge" is modified, in the one case, by an indication of sex and, in the other, by an indication of ethnicity. This implies that, within a given culture, *judge* simply or unqualifiedly speaking is nonfemale (male) and non-Hispanic (white). Using the unmarked "judge" to designate white males and using marked signifiers in the other instances point to the differences of power within the culture. In general, the unmarked signifiers conceal the possibilities of sexual or ethnic bias of the dominant sex and ethnic group, while the marked signifiers insinuate bias (What verdict would you expect from a *woman* judge in a rape case?). Power operates most effectively when it is invisible. Unmarked signifiers are one of the important ways the powerful can exert themselves without being seen. Marking traditionally unmarked signifiers is often an effective way of undermining or challenging the power or authority of those who have traditionally been marginalized; that is, of maintaining the status quo.

Meaning. A term whose multiplicity of meanings is so great as to defy summary. In **semiotics,** there is, however, widespread agreement that *meaning* is not an explanatory term but a term requiring explanation. For an under-

140

standing of meaning, we need to turn to what **signs** are and how they function.

One important semiotic conception of meaning is that translatability provides the key for explaining meaning (see, for example, Claude Levi-Strauss's *Myth and Meaning* and Roman **Jakobson**'s "Sign and System of Language"): The meaning of a sign resides in the possibilities inherent in the sign of being translated into other signs. Another important semiotic approach to this topic is found in Charles S. **Peirce**'s conception of the **interpretant** of a sign: The meaning of a sign is its power to generate a series of interpretants. Since Peirce distinguishes various kinds of interpretants, the meaning of a sign is a complex affair. See also ***Bedeutung,*** **behaviorist theory of meaning, locution, mentalism, reference, usage.**

Mediation. From Latin *mediare,* to be in the middle; *medius,* middle. The process of bringing together things that otherwise would be unconnected; the result of such a process. This notion is important in **semiotics,** since signs perform the **function** of mediation.

When I put on my glasses, they mediate between my eyes and my visual field. When the curtain falls in a theater, it comes—and, thus, in a sense, mediates— between the audience and the performers who only a moment before were visible to it. In both cases there is a process of mediation, of one thing coming between two others. But the results of such a process can be, as the two examples show, quite different. When I put on my glasses, they mediate in such a way as to make accessible what would otherwise be beyond my power to see; but when the curtain falls, it mediates in such a way as to make inaccessible what just moments before was visible to the audience. In most circumstances, the outcome of this process is an open question; whether it brings the mediated things together or cuts them apart can only be ascertained on a case-by-case basis.

Many attempts to define **sign** in its most general sense focus on one or another function (for example, the function of one thing standing for something other than itself, or that of representing an object, or that of generating an **interpretant**). The function of mediating, of bringing together what would otherwise be disparate or unconnected has been proposed as *the* defining trait of anything we might, properly speaking, call a sign. Regarding the highly general and abstract character of many terms in semiotics, see **relatum.**

Medieval. Pertaining to the Middle Ages (the period in Western history from around A.D. 500 to A.D. 1500). Especially in the High (later) Middle Ages, much attention was devoted to **logic.** The treatises resulting from this are of direct and still largely unappreciated relevance to **semiotics.** See also **contemporary, modern, scholastic.**

Mentalism. From *mens,* Latin for mind. The doctrine that **meaning** is exclusively or, at least, primarily something the mind confers on **signs** and **symbols.** More often than not, it is the mind in isolation from other minds that is supposed to be the originator of meaning. In opposition to mentalism, most semioticians maintain that meaning inheres in signs and symbols and also that mind as a subjective phenomenon is itself the result of semiotic processes. See also **antipsychologism, behaviorist theory of meaning, experience, thought.**

Message. Whatever is conveyed or transmitted in a communicational exchange. The message is one of the six dimensions or components of **communication.** In any act of communication, an **addresser** conveys a message to an **addressee.** In order for a message to be conveyed, there must be both a **code** and **channel** (or contact). All messages occur in a **context**. When a communicational exchange is directed toward the message itself, that exchange serves a **poetic** or **aesthetic function**.

Meta-. Prefix meaning beyond or above.

Metalanguage. A language used to talk about another language. The language being talked about is the object language, while the language used to describe, explain, evaluate, etc. the object language is a metalanguage.

Metalingual, metalinguistic. Terms used by Roman **Jakobson** to identify one of the six communicative **functions,** namely, the function by which **communication** is directed toward the **code** or set of codes. Since not all communicational exchanges depend on linguistic codes, it might be more appropriate to call this function meta-semiotic.

Metanarrative. A story or **narrative** constructed or judged to illuminate or even explain other stories; an overarching or all-inclusive story or **discourse** allegedly providing a comprehensive and final perspective. Marxism is sometimes characterized as a theory that offers a metanarrative: The traditional religious stories are, according to this metanarrative, adequately grasped only when they are seen in light of the ongoing struggle against human oppression. According to Marxism, the story of class struggle is the story of stories, the story in light of which the meaning of all other narratives is revealed to us.

Postmodernism has been defined by Jean-François Lyotard as a suspicion of metanarratives. In addition, he argues that since metanarratives are theories purporting to explain the totality of things, they are easily put into the service of totalitarians. History suggests a tragic link between totalizing theories and totalitarian practices. See also **modernity**.

Metaphor. In one sense, a figure of speech in which a word or expression is transferred from its customary domain to an unusual one; in a more general sense, the name for any **trope** or figure of speech.

There is an enormous and still-growing literature on the topic of metaphor. In this literature one encounters widely divergent and heatedly contested accounts of this trope. While its importance to an understanding of language and perhaps also to other systems of signs is virtually conceded by all contributors to this literature, it is difficult to find many other wide areas of agreement. See also **metonymy.**

Metatheory. A theory regarding the formulation and justification of theories—in short, a theory about theories.

Methodeutic. The term used by Charles S. **Peirce** to designate the third and culminating branch of **logic.** For Peirce, logic is a **normative science** divided into three branches: **speculative grammar, critic,** and **speculative rhetoric** or methodeutic. The third branch provides nothing less than a theory of inquiry; Peirce described it as "The Quest of Quests—An Inquiry into the Conditions of the Success of Inquiry (beyond the collection and observation of facts" (CP 5.568n).

Metonymy. A **trope** or figure of speech in which the name of one thing is substituted for the name of something ordinarily associated with it. When it is said that the White House announced its decision today to reject the budget being prepared by Congress, the name of a building is being used metonymically. A **synecdoche,** an important kind of metonymy, involves substituting either the name of a part for the whole or the name of the whole for a part.

Mirror stage. An early stage in the psychological development of a human being (a stage stressed by Jacques

Lacan) in which the young child comes to recognize itself in the mirror.

Modern. In philosophy, a term that generally means post**medieval** and pre**contemporary**. This covers the period roughly from A.D. 1500 to the late nineteenth or early twentieth century. In literary studies, however, modern refers to the twentieth century. See also **Enlightenment, modernity, scholastic.**

Modernity. The constellation of assumptions, values, and attitudes by which the **modern** period is distinguishable from previous epochs (for example, the Middle Ages) and, if such a time has in fact arrived, the postmodern period. The characterization of a period as long and complex as the period from A.D. 1500 to the outbreak of World War I or the discovery of special relativity (or whatever other symbolic event one chooses as marking the close of modernity) is an enormous and controversial undertaking. See also **contemporary, Enlightenment.**

Morphology. A term traditionally used to denote the branch of linguistics devoted to investigating the form or structure of words. In the writings of Luce **Irigaray** and the authors she has influenced, however, morphology means something quite different, the form of our bodily **subjectivity.** This form is engendered in the double sense of coming into being and of being sexually differentiated (female or male).

Morris, Charles (1901–1979). A contemporary American semiotician of considerable importance. "Semiotic has for its goal," in Morris's view, "a general theory of signs in all their forms and manifestations, whether in animals or men, whether normal or pathological, whether linguistic or nonlinguistic, whether personal or social. Semiotic is thus an interdisciplinary enterprise" (1938, 1; quoted in Noth 1990, 49). Morris considered this enterprise to be "both a science among the [other] sciences and an instrument of the sciences" (1938, 2; quoted in Noth 1990, 49). He divided the science of signs into **syntactics** (the study of signs in relationship to other signs), **semantics** (the study of signs in relationship to their objects or denotata), and **pragmatics** (the investigation of signs in relationship to their users—their producers and interpreters).

Motivation vs. **arbitrariness.** Motivation, the term used by Ferdinand de **Saussure** to designate that the link between **signifier** and **signified** is in some respects not completely arbitrary—that there is a motive or "reason" for connecting a particular signifier with a particular signified; arbitrariness, the term used to designate the absence of any such link. For Saussure, **symbols** are **signs** in which the link between signifier and signified is motivated or nonarbitrary. To take his own example, the use of scales to symbolize a court of justice is motivated, for the signifier (the scales) bear a resemblance to what they signify (presumably because in a court the judge or jury weigh evidence) in the way the word "court" does not.

Myth. From Greek *mythos,* story. A term sometimes used in a very broad sense (in fact, in accord with its original meaning in Greek) to designate story (**see narrative**); more often, a word used with a narrower meaning (for example, the story or collection of stories by which a culture or religion defines itself). Claude Levi-Strauss, Roland **Barthes,** and Paul **Ricoeur** have each, though in quite different ways, explored the topic of myth.

Mythos. Greek word for story, often used in contrast

146

to *logos.* The word used by Aristotle in his *Poetics* to designate something at least closely approximating what narratologists today call **plot.**

N

Narrative. A specific kind of **text** or **discourse** in which a **story** of some form is related.

Narrativity. The feature or set of features by which **narrative** is distinguished from other kinds of **text** or **discourse.**

Narratology. The study of **narrative,** frequently undertaken from a structuralist perspective (see **structuralism**) and thus concerned with discovering the grammar of narrative. See also **discourse analysis, Greimas.**

Neologism. A newly coined or invented word. In the course of his investigation of signs, Charles S. **Peirce,** one of the co-founders of contemporary **semiotics,** invented numerous terms. His motivation was the same as that of the physicist who introduced the term *quark*—newly discovered realities merit their own distinctive names. See also **ethics of terminology.**

New Criticism. A significant movement in literary criticism, flourishing in the United States from the late 1930s to the 1950s, marked by its insistence upon the **autonomy** of literary works. Neither the author's intentions nor the reader's reactions to such works were considered by the New Critics relevant to an appreciation and understanding of these works. What they advocated was a close reading of the work itself as a formal structure. In practice, however, New Criticism stopped short of a thoroughgoing formalism. It was a healthy corrective to what at the time of its emergence was, among many literary analysts, an overemphasis on psychological and biographical matters.

In **contemporary** thought, the formalist impulse in literary and, more generally, aesthetic theory and criticism has been strong; New Criticism is but one influential manifestation of this impulse. Almost invariably, preoccupation with artworks as self-contained forms calls forth a reaction: The systematic neglect of **context** is challenged and the human dimensions of art are reaffirmed.

New Historicism. A very recent reaction among literary theorists and others against the perceived ahistoricism of some of the most dominant approaches to textual analysis and criticism (above all, **New Criticism,** archetypal criticism, and **deconstructionism**). The New Historicists are committed to investigating literary texts in light of their historical and political contexts.

Noise. A sound that interferes with, or rules out, the reception of a **message;** more generally, anything that works against a message reaching its destination. It concerns the **channel** of **communication.**

Nomenclature. From Latin *nomen,* name; *nomenclatura,* calling by name, a list of names. The process of naming; the result of this process—the set of names itself.

Early in his *Course on General Linguistics,* Ferdinand de **Saussure** asks: "Why has **semiology** [the study of signs in general] not yet been recognized as an independent science with its own object like all other sciences?" He replies to his own question by noting: "Linguists have been going around in circles: languages, better than anything else, offer a basis for understanding the semiological

148

problem [that is, the problem of understanding "the life of signs within society"]; but language must . . . be studied correctly; heretofore language has almost always been studied in connection with something else . . ." (16). For example, language has been, in accord with "the superficial notion of the general public," seen as "nothing more than a name-giving system"; that is, a nomenclature. In opposition to this notion, Saussure insists that language is *not* a set of names. This denial means at least two things. First, there is more to language than nomenclature: Naming is only one and not even necessarily the most important function of language. Second, and more radically, any language is a system of signs or, more fully, a self-contained system of arbitrary correlations between signifiers and signifieds (for instance, acoustic images and conceptual contents—the phoneme "dog" and the meanings linked to it). This implies that there are no independently existing concepts, let along independently existing things, to which names are attached. Rather, concepts are acquired only through language: "Psychologically our thought—apart from its expression in words—is only a shapeless and indistinct mass" (111). And the world itself is divided up differently by different languages. Hence, on this view, language does not give us names to designate prelinguistically known things; it gives us nothing less than a world. For, apart from language, everything (not only our thought) would be—for us, at least—a shapeless and indistinct mass.

Nominalism. From Latin *nomen*, name. A doctrine concerning the status of **universals.** For the nominalist, individuals alone are real and universals are mere names or sounds of the voice.

Universals are terms predicable (see **predication**) on an indefinite range of objects. One can apply the same term to different things, for instance, *human being* to Plato, Aristotle, Peirce, Saussure, and so on. The ontological status of beings such as Plato and Aristotle is ordinarily assumed to be unproblematic: They are individuals and, as such, undeniably **real** or **actual.** (The ontological status of beings or designata—that is, whatever can be designated or identified—refers to their standing in reality.) But what about the ontological status of universals? What standing in reality do they have? According to nominalism, universal terms are merely vocal sounds or utterances; the only basis they have is in how we speak. In contrast, realists (see **realism**) maintain that at least some universals have a basis in reality. When one says of Plato, Aristotle, and so on that they are human beings, one does so on the basis not simply of a linguistic **convention** but ultimately of some objective feature or features shared by different individuals.

In Charles S. **Peirce**'s writings, nominalism bears a variety of meanings, including the doctrine that existence or actuality is the only mode of being. He rejected nominalism in this and in most of its other senses.

Nonverbal communication. Communication by means other than spoken or written words. Mime and gesture are examples of such communication.

Normative science. A term used by Charles S. **Peirce** to designate one of three philosophical disciplines (**logic,** ethics, and aesthetics or—as he more often spelled it—esthetics) devoted to providing a general theory of deliberative conduct (of human action insofar as it can be regulated by norms and ideals). In one of his descriptions, he characterized logic as the theory of self-controlled **inquiry,** ethics as the theory of self-controlled conduct in general, and aesthetics as an account and justification of the highest good (the ultimate goal of human conduct).

He suggested that the highest good is the continuous growth of concrete reasonableness.

Since Peirce maintained that the study of signs either falls within the scope of logic or is but another name for logic, and since he classified logic as one of the normative sciences, he conceived his investigation of signs as part of normative science.

O

Object. That which stands over against something else; that which confronts one as **other**. This meaning is suggested by the etymology of both the English word "object" (that which throws itself against or in the way) and its German equivalent, *Gegenstand* (that which stands against or is opposed). See also **alterity, difference, otherness.**

Whereas Ferdinand de **Saussure** presented a **dyadic** or two-termed model of the sign (**sign** as an arbitrary correlation between **signifier** and **signified**), Charles S. **Peirce** proposed a triadic or three-termed model. For Peirce, anything properly designated as a sign has an object; moreover, this object is conceived in such a way that it can constrain or guide the process of **semiosis** or sign generation. In other words, whereas Saussure's view of **language** as a self-contained **system** of formal differences suggests something free-floating, Peirce's conception of semiosis suggests something firmly rooted in an objective world. In Saussure's **semiology,** the link between language and reality is severed or, at best, extremely attenuated; in Peirce's

semeiotic, the connection between signs and objects is commonsensically assumed.

Object, immediate vs. **dynamic.** *Immediate* object, the object as it is represented by a sign; in contrast, the *dynamic* object, the object as it really is apart from the way it is represented by this or that sign.

Charles S. **Peirce** introduced this **distinction** into **semiotics.** His motive in drawing this distinction was to provide a means of expressing what he took to be the definitive feature of human knowing—the inescapable possibility of error (see **fallibilism**). While an object or state of affairs might be the way it is represented in some sign (I might say that today the President of the United States declared war against Iraq and, in fact, he did make such a declaration), it might also be misrepresented by a sign. In true statements, the immediate and the dynamic object are one and the same thing; in a false statement, they are different.

One additional aspect of Peirce's dynamic object deserves mention here: This object is a source of constraint on **inquiry** or **interpretation.** There is something to which we can appeal to determine the accuracy of our interpretations or the reliability of our judgments, something that has the power, as it were, to talk back—to say to us "No, I'm not!" in response to our representation that the burner on the stove is cool or the ice on the pond is firm. Of course, we often are not in the position to determine so quickly and decisively whether the immediate object coincides with the dynamic object.

Ostranenie **(***Ostranenye***).** Russian word used by Viktor Shklovsky and other **Russian formalists** to identify the essential function of poetry and possibly other forms of art. The word means "making strange," and Shklovsky used it because he believed that the poetic use of language is designed to defamiliarize us with our world and ourselves, so that we might see them afresh. See also **defamiliarization.**

Other, otherness. That which is other than and usually unassimilable to another (for example, the unconscious is the other of consciousness). See also **alterity, difference, object.**

Other of the other vs. **other of the same.** The terms used by Luce **Irigaray** to distinguish, on the one hand, the way women are coming to be or might be represented by women (the other of the other) and, on the other hand, the way women have been and are still represented by patriarchal systems of **representation.**

P

Pan-. Prefix derived from Greek for *all* or *every*. A panacea is a cure-all, a panoramic view one in which every direction can be seen. See also **pansemiotic.**

Panchronic. From Greek *pan-* and *chronos,* time. A panchronic approach to, say, language is an approach including *every* aspect or *all* dimensions of time. It needs to be understood in reference to **diachronic** and **synchronic.** A diachronic approach focuses on the successive changes undergone by a language over the course of time, while a synchronic approach studies language as a simultaneous system of relations co-existing in the present. Thus, the diachronic concerns time as a succession of changes and the synchronic concerns what occurs simultaneously, not successively. Language might be examined in light of its past (for instance, the present form of a word in light of earlier forms), or it might be investigated in light of its present. A panchronic approach would try to include both the synchronic and the diachronic approaches. Ferdinand de **Saussure** argued against adopting a panchronic approach, insisting strenuously that the study of *langue* (**language**), in contrast to *parole* (**speech** or **discourse**), can only be studied synchronically. In opposition to the Neogrammarians (an influential nineteenth-century school of linguists who contended that the only approach to the study of language is a historical approach), Saussure maintained that the formal object of linguistics is **language** as a **system** fully realized and present at any moment. In other words, he advocated the **synchronic** study of language rather than the **diachronic**—the study of language as something complete in the present rather than something evolving (that is, different now than it was in the past).

Pansemiotic, pansemiotism. The view that everything is, in some manner and measure, a sign. Charles S. **Peirce** went so far as to claim that: "The entire universe . . . is perfused with signs, if it is not composed exclusively of signs" (CP 5.448).

Umberto **Eco** warns against semiotic imperialism, the belief that semiotics provides us with the last word or final truth about anything and everything. He stresses the need to distinguish between two different "hypotheses": the conjecture that everything *must* be studied sub specie semiotica (roughly, from the perspective of semiotics) and the conjecture that everything *can* be investigated from this viewpoint, though with varying degrees of success (1976 22; 27).

Paradigm. In general, pattern, exemplar, or example (especially an outstanding or unproblematic example); more technically, a theoretical, methodological, or heuristic framework. This second, more technical meaning is related to the first, more general one, for such frameworks are universally or at least widely recognized achievements that provide model problems and solutions to a community of investigators.

Paradigmatic vs. **syntagmatic.** See **associative, axis.**

Paradigm shift. The historian and philosopher of science Thomas Kuhn's *The Structure of Scientific Revolution* (1962) itself inaugurated a revolution in the way we have since come to think about science. Kuhn contrasts periods of normal science with phases of conceptual revolution. Kuhn and countless others who have been influenced by him use "paradigm shift" to designate the transition from an established paradigm of scientific research to a new one. Kuhn stressed the extrarational nature of such transitions. This has generated a still-lively controversy regarding the nature of paradigm shifts and the rationality of science itself. See also *coupure epistemologique,* **incommensurability.**

Parapraxis. The technical term for what is ordinarily called a Freudian slip (a slip of the tongue, a mistake in writing, an apparently accidental injury). Freud took these "slips" to be significant: They almost always betray powerful but unconscious motives.

Parole vs. *Langue.* French words meaning, respectively, speech (**discourse**) and **language.**

Parousia. Greek for arrival, presence. In Jacques **Derrida**'s writings, we find a critique of the philosophy (or metaphysics) of **presence.** The history of Western philosophy has been, in one way or another, an attempt to define being in terms of what can be or is fully and finally present. Plato's philosophy is one of the earliest and most influential attempts to conceive being as *parousia* (presence). Christian theology and philosophy represent a later attempt. Anything of which we are aware or about which we can discourse is only partially and fleetingly present—indeed, it is but a **trace** of what is always absent. The **transcendental signified** is one way Derrida identifies the overarching ideal of Western philosophy. Central to his critique of this metaphysics is Derrida's acceptance of the infinite **play** of signifiers and the endless deferral of meaning.

Patrilocation. Location within a patriarchal system.

Peirce, Charles Sanders (1839–1914). An American philosopher who (along with Ferdinand de **Saussure**) founded contemporary semiotics. "I am, as far as I know, a pioneer, or rather a backwoodsman, in the work of clearing and opening up what I call semiotic, that is[,] the doctrine of the essential nature and fundamental varieties of possible semiosis" or sign process (CP 5.488).

Performative utterance. An utterance such as a vow or promise for which, in the appropriate circumstance, the utterance itself entails the performance of a socially recognized act. If I say in a serious tone that I promise to meet you at six o'clock, then the uttering of these words constitutes a promise. See also **constative, nomenclature.**

Perlocution, perlocutionary force. The effect of an utterance upon a listener or reader. J. L. **Austin** distinguishes **locution, illocution,** and perlocution or the locutionary, perloctionary, and illocutionary force of an utterance. If someone says (or utters) the statement "I'm tired," the statement-in-context has a meaning in accord with established usage (or possibly a metaphorical deviation from such usage). This is its *locutionary* force. But, in uttering these words, the speaker might be doing more than revealing a physiological or psychological state—making a request to go home. This would be its *illocution-*

ary force. The effect of the words on the listener might be irritation. This would be the *perlocutionary* force of the utterance. See also **speech act theory.**

Phallocentric, phallocentrism. Phallocentric, characteristic of anything privileging the **phallus** or phallic forms of **discourse** (for example, the hard over the soft, the penetrating over the engulfing); phallocentrism, the tendency to **privilege** the phallus or phallic forms of discourse, **representation,** etc.

Phallus. A symbol of the penis or, more generally, of power conceived in its stereotypically male forms; in Jacques Lacan's writings, a signifier evocative of whatever would overcome the **lack** felt by human **subjects.**

Phaneroscopy. A term Charles S. **Peirce** used to designate a branch of inquiry more commonly called **phenomenology.** Peirce coined this term from the Greek words *phaneron* and *scopy.* The principal task of phaneroscopy is the discovery of universal **categories.** For this reason Peirce often characterized phaneroscopy (or phenomenology) as the doctrine of the categories.

Phatic function. The function of **communication** concerned with determining the state or quality of the **channel** (or contact) through which a **message** is being conveyed. When someone walks up to a microphone and says "Testing—one, two three; testing—one two three," that person's aim is to determine the state or quality of the channel (or contact) of communication. When a message concerns the channel or contact, its function is said to be phatic.

Phenomenon (plural **phenomena**). Appearance; the way things *appear to us* in contrast to **noumena,** things as they *are in themselves,* apart from how they appear to us or any other kind of knower. *Phenomenon* and *noumenon* are thus technical terms for appearance and reality, respectively. *Phenomenon* is also used to designate a specific kind of appearance: one calling for an explanation (see **abduction**).

The German philosopher Immanuel Kant (1724–1804) construed the **distinction** between phenomena and noumena as a **dualism.** Noumena or things-in-themselves are, in principle, unknowable; thus our knowledge is limited to appearances or phenomena. Charles S. **Peirce** rejected this dualism, contending that our acquaintance with the appearances of things provides us with a more or less reliable basis for knowing things themselves.

Phenomenology. A term used by Charles S. **Peirce** to designate a discipline within philosophy (see **phaneroscopy**); also used to denote an important movement in **contemporary** philosophy associated with such thinkers as Edmund Husserl, Maurice Merleau-Ponty, and Roman Ingarden. It might be said that this movement began when Husserl, in opposition to the neo-Kantian suggestion that the reform of philosophy was to be accomplished by going back to Kant, proposed that we go to the things themselves or, more exactly, to the things as they present themselves to our consciousness. In other words, the reform of philosophy required a return to phenomena, a return itself requiring the divestiture of our prejudices and preconceptions. Husserl and Merleau-Ponty themselves undertook investigations of signs, and their general approach and specific inquiries into other matters have had a wide and deep influence.

Phoneme. A unit of sound; the smallest unit of sound in a given **language.** Language conceived as a phonemic system is studied by identifying the most basic units of sound (the phonemes) and the various rules governing the combination of these units. This way of studying the

system of language has exerted in the twentieth century a tremendous influence on the study of other sign systems, such as human culture, myths, and narratives.

A phoneme is a sound with a distinctive function within a given system of **aural** signs (for example, spoken English). The /h/ in *hat* is discernibly different from the /m/ in *mat*. It is a difference that makes a difference for speakers of English, whereas the difference between the ways you and I pronounce /h/ (even though it might be quite noticeable) is a negligible difference. A sound attains the status of a phoneme in a language by virtue of its being a difference that makes a difference, one that allows us to differentiate this from that (this word from that; this meaning from that). From the perspective of **structural linguistics,** any language approached as a system of aural signs is not a mere hodgepodge, or random collection, of sounds that function as phonemes by virtue of their intrinsic qualities; it is truly a **system** whose units (in this case, phonemes) are such by virtue of their opposition to (or difference from) the other units in the system, not by virtue of what they are in themselves. Since such a structuralist approach has proved so fruitful in linguistics (or the study of language), it might also prove fruitful in the investigation of other topics—for example, communicative behavior comprehensively conceived. The first step in a structuralist approach to communicative behavior would be the identification of the most basic unit within the system of such behavior. Pike proposed to call this unit the acteme (see **articulation**).

Phonocentrism. The tendency to **privilege** spoken **language;** that is, to make this form of language central and other forms (in particular, written or inscribed language) marginal or peripheral (see **margin**). (See Sarup 1989, 37ff.) This tendency has been linked by Jacques

Derrida with the metaphysics of **presence** since the illusion of immediacy (of speakers being fully present to one another and also to whatever they are talking about) is supported by the privileging of speech.

Phytosemiotics. The **semiotics** of plants.

Plaisir du texte, **le.** An expression used by the French semiotician Roland **Barthes** to designate the pleasure of the text. Sometimes this pleasure seems to be construed in erotic and even autoerotic terms. See also **bliss, texts of.**

Play. In the writings of Jacques **Derrida** and other **deconstructionists,** the thematic of play is extremely prominent. One form this takes is the prominence of puns (plays on words). Another is the insistence upon the play of **signifiers** (the insistence that the meaning of a text is not fixed or even stable, but open to novel and often ironic developments). Our ordinary understanding of play as a spontaneous, delightful, and intrinsically motivated activity informs, to some extent, the usages of these authors. Also evident here is the influence of Friedrich Nietzsche, the nineteenth-century German philosopher who confessed "I do not know any other way of associating with great tasks than *play.*"

Plot/story. See **story/plot.**

Plurisignation. See **ambiguity.**

Poetic function of language. See **aesthetic function.**

Poiesis. Greek term for making, used in contrast to both *praxis* (doing or practice) and *theoria.*

Poinsot, John (1589–1644). A very early modern author who appears to have been the first to undertake a systematic and comprehensive study of signs. John Deely's work on (including his translations of) John Poinsot's writings provides us with invaluable resources for understanding and appreciating the contributions of this important early semiotician.

Poly-. Prefix from the Greek word for many.

Polyfunctional. Having many or at least several **functions.** See **architecture, fashion.**

Polysemy. Having many or at least several **meanings.**

Positivism. The doctrine put forth by Auguste Comte (1798–1857) at the center of which is the contention that positive (or scientific) knowledge is destined to replace philosophical (or metaphysical) speculation, just as philosophical speculation earlier replaced religious (or theological) ideas; more generally, a term used to designate the position or attitude of those who advocate using the methods of science. Today this term is often used disparagingly, since many contemporary authors contend that scientific methods have only limited applicability. See also **logical positivism, scientificity.**

Postmodernism. A term widely used to designate the sensibility characteristic of advanced capitalist countries since at least the 1960s. In *The Postmodern Condition,* Jean-François Lyotard writes: "Simplifying to the extreme, I define *postmodern* as incredulity toward **metanarratives**" (1979 [1984], xxiv).

Poststructuralism. A **contemporary** theoretical movement in which certain structuralist positions (most notably, the view of language as a system of differences) are retained and some central structuralist aspirations (above all, the desire to transform our studies of language, literature, culture, etc. into sciences) are rejected.

Postulate. Like both an **axiom** and a **hypothesis,** a **proposition** from which other truths are derived or on which **inquiry** is based. While a postulate in the strict sense lacks the certainty of an axiom, it is more than a merely provisional assumption or hypothesis.

Pragmaticism. A term Charles S. **Peirce** introduced to distinguish his own version of **pragmatism** from other versions. In 1905, Peirce observed that "the word [pragmatism] begins to be met with occasionally in the literary journals, where it gets abused in the merciless way that words have to expect when they fall into literary clutches" (CP 5.414). Finding his "bantling 'pragmatism' " so promoted, he felt that it was time to kiss his child good-by and relinquish it to its higher destiny. To indicate the original definition, he begged "to announce the birth of the word 'pragmaticism,' which is ugly enough to be safe from kidnappers." In coining this term, Peirce was following a rule he himself laid down in his **ethics of terminology.** There he suggested that, "just as is done in chemistry, it might be wise to assign fixed meanings to certain prefixes and suffixes. For example, it might be agreed, perhaps, that the prefix *prope-* should mark a broad and rather indefinite extension of the meaning of the term to which it was prefixed; the name of a doctrine would naturally end in *-ism*, while *-icism* might mark a more strictly defined acception of that doctrine . . ." (CP 5.413). Thus, when Peirce states that "pragma*ticism* is a species of *prope*-positivism" (CP 5.423; emphasis added), he is claiming that pragmatism in one of its stricter or narrower senses is, in a broad and somewhat indefinite way, a form of **positivism.**

Pragmatics. A term used by Charles **Morris** to designate that branch of **semiotics** devoted to investigating the relationship between **signs** and their various users (that is, producers and interpreters). See also **semantics, syntactics.**

Pragmatism. A philosophical doctrine formulated and defended by Charles S. **Peirce,** William James, John

Dewey, George Herbert Mead, and C. I. Lewis. It was originally formulated by Peirce as a maxim for how to make our ideas clear (see **clarity, grades of**). It evolved into a theory of **meaning** and, later, into a theory of truth. As a theory of meaning, pragmatism insists upon the necessity of interpreting our utterances in terms of their conceivable bearing upon our conduct. As a theory of truth, it proposes that we conceive truth in terms of such notions as what facilitates our commerce with experience. See also **pragmaticism.**

Praxis. Greek word for practice, used in contrast to *theoria,* on the one hand, and *poiesis* on the other. See also **discursive practices.**

Predicate, predication. From Latin *predicare,* to say of. A predication is what is said of something; or the process. In the simple assertion "Peter Carlo is delightful," the quality of being delightful is being predicated (said) of a young child. The word or expression said of something or someone is called the *predicate* (here "delightful" is the predicate); the object or being about which something is being said is the *subject* (the boy bearing the name Peter Carlo).

Prescissive. The term used by Charles S. **Peirce** to designate the form of the process by which we focus upon certain aspects of a phenomenon to the disregard of other aspects. See also **abstraction, hypostatic abstraction.**

Presence, metaphysics of. An expression introduced by Jacques **Derrida** and widely adopted to designate the allegedly dominant orientation of Western thought, an orientation in which the ultimate goal or highest realization of thought or consciousness is self-presence or some other form of presence.

Primary process. A psychoanalytic term used to

identify any one of a number of processes by which the unconscious (in Freud's earlier writings) or the **id** (in his later) seeks satisfaction for its repressed desires and wishes.

Private language. A term used by Ludwig **Wittgenstein** to designate, oxymoronically, a system of signs accessible to and usable by an isolated language-user. For Wittgenstein and numerous other prominent contributors to **semiotics,** all languages are in principle intersubjective; a system of completely private signs would not merit the name *language*. Hans-Georg Gadamer, a representative of **hermeneutics,** makes just this point when he asserts that "Whoever speaks a language that no one else understands does not speak. To speak means to speak *to* someone" (1976, 65). Only that which is, in principle, communicable to others deserves to count as a language.

Privilege, privileged. Privileging, the activity by which something is granted a largely unacknowledged and often undue preference; privileged, the status of being so preferred. *Privilege* and its cognates are prominent terms in the vocabulary of **deconstructionists** and **postmodernists.** The goal of such thinkers is characteristically to call into question the traditionally privileged term in some rigidly fixed hierarchy; for example, reason versus emotion.

Problematique. French word used to identify something that poses a problem or generates a difficulty or, more likely, an array of difficulties; a more or less related set of problems characteristic of a particular field of **inquiry** (for example, the definition of sexual differences for such fields as anthropology and psychoanalysis).

Proper. A term often used in an intentionally ambiguous way (see **ambiguity**), suggesting what is in conformity with the the Law of the Father (the constraints and inhibitions central to patriarchy), what bears the name of the father (one's proper name), and what can be appropriated or made one's own (usually understood as made the same).

Proposition. That which is expressed or conveyed in a statement, in contrast to the both the **assertion** and the manner or media of expression.

Propositional attitude. The attitude or stance one takes toward a **proposition** (for example, doubt or affirmation).

Proxemics. The **semiotics** of space. This branch of semiotics was originally developed by Edward T. Hall in connection with cultural anthropology.

Psychoanalysis. A therapeutic and theoretical approach that stresses the importance of the **unconscious** and explores the mechanisms or processes by which the unconscious operates. A number of highly influential contemporary semioticians (most prominently Jacques **Lacan,** Julia **Kristeva,** and Luce **Irigarary**) are not only psychoanalytically inspired theorists but also trained psychoanalysts.

Q

Qualisign. A type of **sign** or **sign function** in which a quality serves as **a sign vehicle.** According to Charles S. **Peirce,** signs may be considered (1) in reference to themselves, that is, to their sign vehicles, (2) in reference to their **objects,** and (3) in reference to their **interpretants.** By considering signs in reference to its sign vehicle, Peirce derived the trichotomy of qualisign, **sinsign,** and **legisign.** (By considering them in reference to their objects, he derived the trichotomy of **icon, index,** and **symbol.** Finally, by examining them in relation to their interpretants, he established the classification of rheme, dicent, and argument.) A sign vehicle might be a quality, in which case it is a qualisign; or it might be an individual object or event, in which case it is sinsign; or, finally, it might be a law, regularity, **habit,** or **general,** in which case it is a legisign.

R

Ratio. Latin for **reason** or rationality. As the expression "rational animal" implies, the human species has been defined in terms of its possession of reason or rationality. In addition, ratio has been used as one of the divine names (that is, one of the terms used to characterize God). It would be difficult to exaggerate the status and importance granted to reason in the dominant traditions of Western thought, especially philosophy. This status, however, has been challenged throughout history, perhaps never more intensely and variously than in **contemporary** times. Deconstructionism and feminism are two influential movements contesting the traditional place and conceptions of reason. See also *logos,* **logocentricism.**

Rationalism. In a very general sense, a commitment to reason; in a narrower sense, the doctrine that reason in and of itself possesses the capacity to know reality. In the general sense, then, the rationalist is the defender or champion of reason. *Rationalism* is often used more narrowly to designate the position that reason alone—that is, reason apart from experience—is able to discover truths about the world. In this sense, rationalism is opposed to **empiricism** (the doctrine that all knowledge of ourselves and our world is based on experience).

Reader. The decoder or interpreter of a text, verbal or otherwise. In some important currents of **contemporary** literary criticism and theory, attention has shifted from both **texts** and **authors** to readers. As part of this shift, the image of readers as consumers of fixed meanings is replaced by the view of them as producers of open-ended texts. See also **reader-response theory, reading.**

Readerly. The word ordinarily used to translate *lisible,* the French term used by Roland **Barthes** to identify a certain kind of **text.** See also **writable** or **writerly text.**

Reader-response theory. A **contemporary** movement in literary criticism and theory highlighting the response of readers to texts rather than to the allegedly objective features of literary works. Reader-response theory is not so much a specific doctrine as a general reorientation toward literary texts. It involves a refusal and an invitation: a refusal to conceive texts as self-contained entities and an invitation to readers to focus on the ways texts elicit responses (put otherwise, the ways texts act on readers and, in turn, readers respond to texts). The meaning of a text does not inhere in the text itself but emerges in the set of responses making up the process of reading. Wolfgang Iser's *The Act of Reading* (1978) and Stanley Fish's *Is There a Text in This Class?* (1980) are two influential formulations of the reader-response approach. Sometimes *reception theory* is used as a synonym for reader-response theory, but perhaps even more often this expression is used in a narrower sense to designate the reception aesthetics put forth by Hans Robert Jauss.

Reading. The process of decoding the message of a

verbal text; metaphorically, the process of interpreting the meaning of any text, verbal or otherwise. Though *reading* may designate the process of grasping a simple, straightforward message, in semiotic writings this term usually signifies the activity of deciphering complex, labyrinthine texts.

Real, the. A term used by Jacques **Lacan** to designate one of the three orders or registers within which human beings operate. In contrast to both the **imaginary** and the **symbolic,** the real is what absolutely resists symbolization. In this respect, it is similar to Immanuel Kant's notion of **noumena** (or things-in-themselves).

Realism. In literary and art criticism, a mode of representation that conveys the impression of faithfully depicting its subject; in philosophy, a term used to designate several distinct positions. In contrast to **nominalism,** *realism* designates the doctrine that **universals** are real. This doctrine is sometimes called scholastic realism, for the controversy regarding the status of universals was an important one among medieval (or **scholastic**) thinkers. In contrast to one sense of idealism, *realism* signifies the position that the objects of knowledge have a standing or reality apart from our consciousness or knowledge of them. Finally, in contrast to **anti-realism,** it refers to the position that it makes sense to ask whether our **representations** of things accurately represent the things themselves. For the anti-realist, it is pointless or worse to inquire about this.

Reality. The mode of being ordinarily defined in contrast to illusion or figment. Charles S. **Peirce** defined reality in terms of **inquiry:** The real is that which the community of inquirers, given an indefinite time, would eventually discover (see, for example, CP 5.311).

Reason. The name for a capacity or set of capacities traditionally supposed to distinguish *homo sapiens* from all other species of animals. Reason has been defined in terms of various capacities, most notably the capacity to form universal or general conceptions, to represent reality, to draw inferences (especially in a self-critical and self-controlled way), and to be objective or disinterested. See also *logos,* **logocentrism, ratio.**

Reception theory. A term used, in a broad sense, as a synonym for **reader-response theory** and, in a narrower sense, as the name for the approach outlined by the literary historian Hans Robert Jauss. Jauss's approach is distinguished from other reader-response theories by its greater emphasis upon the historical and public (or communal) features of aesthetic reception.

Recit. French term used in **narratology** to designate the narrative text itself, in contrast to both the story and narration (the process of storytelling).

Reductionism. The tendency to explain complex phenomena as though they were nothing but disguised instances of simpler phenomena; also the tendency to reduce what is higher to what is lower. The attempt to interpret the quest for truth as nothing but a bid for power is seen by some as an example of reductionism. See also **irreducibility.**

Reference. The range of **objects** to which a **sign** refers or points, in contrast to what a sign means or signifies. The reference *semiotician* includes Charles S. **Peirce,** Ferdinand de **Saussure,** Charles **Morris,** Roland **Barthes,** and the like; these are some of the beings to whom this sign refers. In contrast, the **meaning** of *semiotician* is anyone who investigates, especially in a self-conscious way, the nature and properties of signs. It is possible for a sign to have meaning but not reference; for example, the expression "the present king of France" makes sense even though there is no person to whom it points. See also *Bedeutung,* object.

Reference, inscrutability of. The inability to determine the reference of an utterance or some other sign.

Referent. That to which a **sign** (for example, a statement) refers; the **object** or range of objects to which a sign applies. See also **Bedeutung, reference.**

Relatum (plural **relata**). Latin word for anything insofar as it is related to something else; the term of, or item in, a relationship. For Ferdinand de **Saussure,** a **sign** is essentially a relationship between a **signifier** and a **signified;** signifier and signified are thus the relata in the sign relation.

Because **semiotics** strives to be an all-inclusive theory of signs, it is forced to ever higher levels of **abstraction** and generality. For example, in order to arrive at a conception of the sign *in general,* it abstracts from the differences between spoken and written words and, beyond this, from the differences between verbal and nonverbal signs. In order to frame these abstractions, semiotics is forced to use extremely general terms, such as relatum and **mediation.** It needs words that can meaningfully stretch across a wide range of diverse phenomena. The drive to construct highly abstract models of the sign relation or function is counterbalanced by the drive to develop finely nuanced typologies (or classifications) of signs. While the models are designed to exhibit the *unity* amid the diverse kinds of signs, the typologies are constructed to illuminate the *diversity* present in the semiotic realm.

Replica. Copy or reproduction of a sign; synonym for **token.** If marks or sounds or other perceptible forms (for example, the letters in Braille) were not reproducible or

170

replicable, they could not function as signs. See also **iterability, legisign, type/token.**

Representamen. A term proposed by Charles S. **Peirce** to designate **sign** in the broadest possible sense (see, for example, CP 2.274). He proposed this term because he believed that the English word "sign" and most, if not all, of its equivalents in English and other languages were too closely tied to a **mentalist** understanding of the sign. According to this understanding, the **interpretant** of a sign is something mental (for example, a concept). In opposition to this understanding, Peirce suggested that the interpretants of some signs are not mental (for example, the plant turning toward the sun). See also **mentalism.**

Representation. The process by which one thing stands for another (see **stare pro,** *aliquid stat pro aliquo*) or by which it is presented, depicted, or portrayed in some fashion; the result of such a process. While representation has been taken as the essential function of signs, this view has been challenged by some highly influential contemporary authors (for instance, Michel Foucault and Jacques **Derrida**).

Representation, system of. In general, a **system** of **signs** making possible the **representation** of events, **objects,** and persons. Any natural language (for example, English or French) would be an example of such a system. In contemporary **semiotics,** the biases inherent in systems of representation have become a focus of attention. The work of feminists such as Luce **Irigaray** offers an illustration of this.

Retroduction. A term used by Charles S. **Peirce** to designate the process of **inference** by which **hypotheses** are generated. See also **abduction.**

Rezeptionsasthetik. German word meaning "reception-aesthetics." See also **reception theory.**

Rhematic sign, rheme. A term introduced by Charles S. **Peirce** to designate a specific kind of **sign,** namely, one which has a qualitative possibility for its **interpretant** (see, for example, CP 2.250). Peirce derived the **trichotomy** of rheme, **dicent,** and **argument** by considering a sign in reference to the nature of its interpretant. This threefold classification at least roughly corresponds to the more traditional trichotomy of concept, statement, and argument.

Rhetoric. A term used to designate, in ancient times, the literary art of persuasion and, in contemporary **semiotics,** persuasion by any and all semiotic means. One of the principal concerns of classical rhetoric was the identification and analysis of the various kinds of **tropes** (or figures of speech).

Rhetorical figure. Figure of speech; **trope.**

Russian formalism. A **contemporary** movement in literary theory and analysis that stressed the **autonomy** of art works and literary texts. It arose in Russia around 1915 but was condemned under Stalin as an intolerable form of bourgeois decadence. Viktor Shklovsky, Boris Eikhenbaum, and Roman **Jakobson** were the most prominent figures in this movement. A principal concern of the Russian formalists was to define literariness, that is, the set of conventions and devices that distinguishes the literary use of language from its other uses (especially its everyday use). These theorists also proposed that the chief function of literary texts is **defamiliarization:** The function of such texts is to induce a dislocation so that we might see afresh some aspect of our lives or our world. Finally, they clearly distinguished in their investigations of **narrative** between **plot** (*sjuket*) and **story** (*fabula*). In part, **structuralism** grew out of Russian formalism.

S

Sapir–Whorf hypothesis. A **hypothesis** put forth by Edward Sapir and Benjamin Whorf regarding the role of the language we speak in determining the shape and character of the world we inhabit. Most people assume that the world is simply there, apart from the language and other systems of representation we use. Sapir and Whorf challenged this assumption, proposing that the world we inhabit is largely due to the languages we use. The world is not simply there, but is always encountered through the means of symbolization provided by language and presumably other culturally inherited systems of representation.

Saussure, Ferdinand de (1857–1913). The founder of modern linguistics and (along with Charles S. **Peirce**) the co-founder of contemporary **semiotics,** a field of inquiry he dubbed *semiologie*. In his *Course in General Linguistics,* Saussure announced: "*A science that studies the life of signs within society* is conceivable; it would be part of social psychology and consequently of general psychology; I shall call it *semiology* (from Greek *semeion* 'sign'). Semiology would show what constitutes signs, what laws govern them. Since the science does not yet exist, no one can say what it would be; but it has a right to existence, a place staked out in advance" (1916 [1966], 16). The influence of Saussure on the study of signs has been enormous. There is, however, an independent tradition of semiotic research rooted in Peirce's lifelong devotion to formulating a truly general theory of signs. While Saussure stresses the **arbitrariness** of the sign, Peirce emphasizes its triadicity. In addition, Saussure's approach to the study of linguistic and other signs is based on a series of **dichotomies** (for instance, **signifier/signified; *langue/parole*; synchronic/diachronic; syntagmatic/ paradigmatic**), whereas Peirce's approach involves numerous **trichotomies** (**sign-object-interpretant;** and **icon-index-symbol**). This formal difference is deep and important.

Scholastic. Pertaining to the most important thinkers during the Middle Ages (the period in Western history from around A.D. 500 to around A.D. 1500, who were almost always associated with universities. For this reason they are often called Schoolmen and their thought is identified as scholastic. There are to be found, especially in their writings on logic, discussions directly relevant to **semiotics.**

Science, method of. An expression used by Charles S. **Peirce** to designate a specific method of **inquiry** (or way of fixing **beliefs**). In contrast to the methods of tenacity, authority, and apriority, the method of science supposes that there are real events and objects to which our representations may or may not conform. For Peirce, then, the **hypothesis** of there being something real distinguishes science from other ways of fixing beliefs. For him, **reality** is that which may be other than you or I or any other inquirer happens to think; but it is also what would be discovered in the indefinite long run by the community of inquirers. So defined, reality is possibly other than what we take it to be but ultimately accessible to our understanding. To suppose that there are such realities makes possible a form of inquiry open to revision and self-correction. See also **agreeableness to reason, method of; authority, method of; belief; inquiry.**

Scientia. Latin for science or knowledge. In medieval writings, designates the demonstrative knowledge of things through their causes.

Scientificity. The quality, form or status of science understood not in the medieval sense of *scientia* but in the modern sense of experimental inquiry. Because of the prestige accorded the sciences, especially natural sciences, **contemporary** contributors to disciplines such as philosophy, **semiotics,** and even literary criticism have tried to transform their disciplines into sciences. Especially in recent decades, however, there appears to be a growing awareness that, in some cases at least, the drive toward scientificity is misguided. Among the contributors to semiotics, there is no clear consensus regarding the status and character of their own discipline.

Scriptible. French word usually translated **writerly,** though sometimes left untranslated as a way of acknowledging its origin in the writings of the French semiotician Roland **Barthes.**

Sebeok, Thomas Albert (b. 1920). A major twentieth-century semiotician whose two main contributions are (1) his work as editor for various publications in the field and (2) the cumulative impact his numerous writings have had in broadening the scope of semiotics to include the biosphere.

Secondness. One of Charles S. **Peirce**'s three universal **categories.** By means of secondness, Peirce is calling attention to opposition or reaction, to the brute fact of one thing standing *over against* another. The best example of pure secondness would be two things colliding—getting unexpectedly hit in the back of the head, or

175

pushing against something resisting one's exertions. In taking secondness to be a universal category, Peirce is suggesting that it is omnipresent: Wherever we go, we encounter resistance or opposition, though it is often so mild as to be, for most purposes, entirely negligible. Secondness is close to what today is often called **otherness** or **alterity.** See also **firstness** and, especially, **thirdness.**

Semanteme. Synonym for **sememe,** a unit of meaning; a linguistic element that itself expresses a concept and, in turn, is combinable with other such elements.

Semantic. Relating to **meaning** or **signification;** more narrowly, concerned with the relationship between **signs** and their **objects.**

Semantics. The study of **meaning.** As used by **Charles Morris,** that branch of **semiotics** devoted to studying the relationship between **signs** and their **objects** or, more technically, between **sign vehicles** and their designata (those things these vehicles designate). See also **pragmatics, syntactics.**

Sematology. One of the various names for a general study of **signs,** thus a synonym for **semiotics.**

Semeiotic. The way Charles S. **Peirce** often spelled the word designating the general theory of **signs;** thus, a synonym for what is more commonly called **semiotics.** Sometimes *semeiotic* is used today to differentiate Peirce's or a Peircean approach to the study of signs from other approaches (for example, a Saussurean orientation). Likewise, **semiology** is sometimes used to distinguish Ferdinand de **Saussure**'s or a Saussurean orientation from other orientations.

Seme, sememe. A unit of meaning; more narrowly, the smallest unit of meaning. In **structural linguistics,** sememes are explained in terms of an analogy with **phonemes.** That is, they are units defined in terms of a system of relationships, in particular, oppositions. This view of meaning is holistic; it locates meaning, first and foremost, in language as a system of oppositions rather than in the individual units themselves. The vocable "*bat*" contributes to the working of language not because of its intrinsic qualities but because of its discernible difference from "*cat*," "*mat*," "*hat*," etc. As a constituent of language, a phoneme attains its identity through its differences with other phonemes. Analogously, so do sememes.

Semiogenesis. The genesis or evolution of sign use on the part of some animal species; more narrowly, the evolution of nonlinguistic signs on the part of Homo sapiens. In this narrower sense, semiogenesis is recognized as a process beginning much earlier than **glottogenesis** (the evolution of a phonemic language). Glottogenesis is thought to have begun around fifty thousand years ago, while semiogenesis is presumably as old as the human species itself.

Semiology. A name for the general theory of signs; *semiologie,* the term apparently coined by Ferdinand de **Saussure** to designate the science of signs in general.

Semeion (plural **Semeia**). Greek for **sign.** From very early (beginning with Hippocrates and Parmenides in the fifth century B.C.), *semeion* was used as a synonym for *tekmerion* (evidence, proof, or symptom). In the writings of some ancient Greek authors (for instance, **Aristotle** in several texts), *semeia* are distinguished from *symbola*. The paradigm *semeion* was a medical symptom (for example, spots); the paradigm *symbolum*, a linguistic expression. There is an intrinsic or natural connection between a *semeion* (or sign) and what it signifies; in contrast, there is only a contingent or conventional link between a *symbolum* and what it symbolizes. But, as in contemporary English, this distinction between sign and symbol was in ancient Greek usage not always clearly or consistently drawn.

Semiosis. A term originally used by Charles S. **Peirce** to designate any sign action or sign process; in general, the activity of a **sign.** It is commonly supposed that signs are instruments used by humans and also other animals: In themselves, they are thought to be inert and thus ineffectual. *Semiosis* is often used in such a way as to challenge this perspective, for it signifies an inherently dynamic process over which human sign-users exert no or at most limited control. In other words, signs are not mere instruments: They exert an **agency** of their own.

For Peirce, semiosis is an irreducibly triadic process in which an **object** generates a sign of itself and, in turn, the sign generates an **interpretant** of itself. This interpretant in its turn generates a further interpretant, ad infinitum. Thus semiosis is a process in which a potentially endless series of interpretants is generated.

The semiotic/the symbolic. The semiotic, a term used by Julia Kristeva to designate the rhythms and energies ("pulsions") preceding and transcending the symbolic order; the symbolic, a term used by her to designate the social order into which all human beings are initiated as a condition for becoming speaking subjects. The symbolic order is embodied in such institutions as language, law, morality, and religion. Before being initiated into this order, the infant (etymologically, the speechless one) is caught up in a play of forces and drives; even after he or she has been subjected to the constraints of this order, this play can be detected. Thus the semiotic points to a source of anarchic energies, while the symbolic points to the restrictions of the social order. The semiotic prompts transgressions, whereas the social demands conformity. In any actual *enonciation,* the spontaneous promptings of semiotic drives and the internalized constraints of the symbolic order intersect.

Semiotics. The study or doctrine of **signs,** sometimes supposed to be a **science** of signs; the systematic investigation of the nature, properties, and kinds of sign, especially when undertaken in a self-conscious way.

The study of signs has a long and rich history. As a self-conscious and distinct branch of **inquiry,** however, it is a **contemporary** undertaking flowing from two independent research traditions. One tradition can be traced to Charles S. **Peirce,** an American philosopher and the originator of **pragmatism;** the other can be traced to Ferdinand de **Saussure,** a Swiss linguist who is generally recognized as the founder of contemporary linguistics and the major inspiration for **structuralism.**

Semiotic web. A metaphor used by Thomas A. **Sebeok** to describe our **experience.** Experience is a web woven out of signs and used to catch various objects in our *Umwelt* (or surroundings) for the sake of our survival and flourishing.

Semeiotikos. Greek word for one who interprets or divines the meaning of signs. For classical Greek philosophers, the physician provided a paradigm (outstanding example) of a *semeiotikos.* Galen of Pergamum (139–199), himself a famous physician, understood diagnosis to be a process of *semeiosis,* of sign interpretation. See also **semiosis.**

Sender. One who sends or conveys a **message,** thus a synonym for **addresser,** It is a name for one of the six essential features of any **communication.**

Sign. A term defined traditionally as *aliquid stat pro aliquo* (something that stands for something else). The term itself, apart from any specific meaning, is usually used by semioticians as an all-encompassing or all-inclusive term. **Symbols, icons, myths, texts,** etc. are all signs or systems of signs. In other words, sign is used as an umbrella term—a term under which a host of subtypes huddle.

According to Ferdinand de **Saussure,** a sign is an arbitrary correlation between a **signifier** and a **signified** (for example, an acoustic image and its corresponding concept). A modified version of this **dyadic** model was offered by Louis **Hjelmslev** and adopted by numerous contemporary semioticians, especially in Europe. In it, a sign is the arbitrary correlation of an **expression** plane and a **content** plane. In contrast to such models, Charles S. **Peirce** proposed a **triadic** conception: A sign is anything that stands for something (called its **object**) in such a way as to generate another sign (its **interpretant**).

Signal. A specific type of sign usually characterized as calling for an immediate response. In this sense, the stop sign at the end of an exit off the highway might more properly be called a stop signal (we do in fact speak of traffic signals). Its function is to call for an immediate response—here and now (that is, at the moment one reaches it). Failure to do so can result in another sort of signal—the siren and gestures of a state trooper.

Signans/signatum. Signans, a Latin term ordinarily translated **signifier;** *signatum,* a Latin term ordinarily translated **signified.** See also *signum.*

Sign function. A term sometimes used (for instance, by Umberto **Eco)** as a rough equivalent of **sign.** The motivation to prefer *sign function* to *sign* is that the term *function* suggests something dynamic and (in the judgment of Eco) flexible. Whatever acts like a sign, or is taken to be a sign, does so by virtue of some function (for example, the function of standing for something other than itself or that of mediating between two things that would otherwise be disparate or unconnected). And the same thing can perform different functions in different contexts and even in the same context. See also **mediation, aliquid stat pro aliquo**.

Signifiant. French word almost always translated **signifier**. *Signifiant* is the word Ferdinand de **Saussure** used to identify one side of the sign (or *signe*, a "two-sided psychological entity").

Signification. The process by which **signs** and thus **meanings** are generated or produced. See also *enonciation*.

Significs. Lady Victoria **Welby's** name for "the study of the nature of significance in all its forms and relations" (1911, vii), thus a synonym for what today is more commonly called semiotics. She also proposed *sensifics* as a name for this field of study.

Signifie. French word almost always translated **signified**.

Signified. One of the essential correlates of the **sign** as defined by Ferdinand de **Saussure**. For him, a sign is an arbitrary correlation between a **signifier** and a signified. The signifier calls attention to something other than itself; the signified is the recipient of that attention. The signifier is the perceptual component of the sign (the differences in sound perceptible to the ear), whereas the signified is the conceptual component (the meaning conveyed by means of the sound). Among readers of English, the three marks D-O-G have been correlated to, or linked with something furry, four-legged, etc. These marks serve as a signifier, while the **object** or **concept** has the status of a signified. See also **arbitrariness**.

Signifier. One of the essential correlates of the **sign** as defined by Ferdinand de **Saussure**. In recent years, the status of the signifier has been elevated and that of the signified lowered. The notion of **language,** at least implicit in Saussure's writings, as a self-contained whole leaves problematic the status of the signified.

Signum. Latin for **sign.** Roman **Jakobson** used *signum* as a synonym for Ferdinand de **Saussure's** *signe.* Writing in French, Saussure defined *signe* as a *signifiant* correlated to a *signifie* (a signifier correlated to a signified); translated into Latin, we have a *signum* resulting from the correlation of a *signans* (signifier) with a *signatum* (signified).

Signum ad placitum. Conventional signs.

Sign Vehicle. That component of a sign by which the **sign function** is fulfilled or at least taken up. Since a sign is ordinarily thought to convey a message, that component of it which is most directly responsible for this conveyance is appropriately called a vehicle (a term meaning, after all, a means of transport or conveyance).

Since the term **sign** may be taken to include its **object** as part of itself (as the object is, for example, in Charles S. **Peirce's** triadic or three-termed definition of the sign), confusion can arise regarding what *sign* itself signifies, for we ordinarily think of signs as distinct and perhaps even separable from their objects. Does *sign* signify in, for example, Peirce's definition, the whole constellation of sign-object-interpretant, or just one item in this constellation? To clarify this matter, it is sometimes proposed that we use *sign* to designate the entire constellation and *sign vehicle* to identify one of the correlates.

Sinn. German word ordinarily translated "sense" or "meaning" and contrasted with **reference (*Bedeutung*).** For the sake of clarity, it is often helpful to distinguish the *Sinn* (or meaning) of a word or expression from its *Bedeutung* (or reference). The two expressions "Morning Star" and "Evening Star" mean something quite different (as different as day and night or, at least, dawn and dusk); they, however, refer to the same planet: Venus.

Sinsign. A term used by Charles S. **Peirce** to designate a specific type of **sign,** one in which an individual event or object serves as the **sign vehicle.** If there is a knock on the door announcing the arrival of guests, this rap is a sinsign. More accurately, it is a **dicent, index**ical sinsign. It is a dicent (or dicisign) since it in effect performs the function of an asserted proposition ("The guests have arrived"). It is indexical since there is an actual, physical connection between the sign vehicle and its object (the knocking sound and the guests announcing their arrival by means of knocking). Finally, it is a sinsign because the knocks as they are occurring here and now—the sounds in their individuality—serve as the sign vehicle.

Signs might be considered in themselves; that is, in terms of what the sign vehicle is in itself, for different things play the role of signs. When a quality plays this role, we have (in Peirce's usage) a **qualisign;** when something general or lawlike performs this function, we have a **legisign;** and when an individual or actual existent assumes the role of sign, we have a sinsign. The **trichotomy** of qualisign, sinsign, and legisign is part of an intricate classification of signs devised by Peirce, for he also considers the sign in its relation to its **object** and in its relation to its **interpretant.** Each of these considerations yields a trichotomy. In relation to its **dynamic** object, a sign may be either an **icon,** an **index,** or a **symbol.** In relation to its interpretant, it may be either a **rheme,** a **dicisign,** or an **argument.** Peirce doesn't stop here: He goes on to explore the possibilities of combining the specific types of sign or, perhaps better, **sign function** identified in these three trichotomies.

Sjuzet (suzet, syuzhet). Russian word used by the Russian formalists to designate the **plot** of a **narrative** in contrast to the events making up the **story** (*fabula*).

Skeptic, skepticism. The skeptic is, etymologically, the inquirer or questioner—one disposed to ask questions or raise doubts. This term is, however, often used in a different and stronger sense by philosophers. The term might mean a person who denies the possibility of knowing anything at all. Skepticism, then, would be the doctrine expressing this denial: Knowledge is unattainable. This term should not be confused with **fallibilism.** It is one thing to say that we might be mistaken at every turn; it is quite another to say that we at no point can know anything at all. The problem of skepticism—of what to say in response to the skeptic in the strong sense—has been a central concern of Western philosophy during its **modern** period and remains a debated issue among **contemporary** philosophers. Some semioticians suppose that an account of knowledge in explicitly semiotic terms will show a way around the Syclla of skepticism and the Charybdis of dogmatism.

Speculative grammar. A branch of **logic** as conceived by Charles S. **Peirce.** Ordinarily logic is defined as the study of **arguments** or **inference.** But Peirce takes this study to be but one part of logic, a part he calls **critic.** In addition to critic, the task of the logicians concerns investigating the processes and forms of meaning on the one hand and inquiry on the other. Speculative grammar is the name for the inquiry into the processes and forms of meaning; that is, into sign actions (see **semiosis**) and sign functions; **speculative rhetoric** or **methodeutic** is the name for the theory of inquiry.

Speculative rhetoric. A term used by Charles S. **Peirce** to designate the third and culminating part of

logic. He also called this branch of logic **methodeutic.** See also **speculative grammar.**

Speech. The term most often used to translate *parole* in contrast to *langue.* Language is the system making communication possible, whereas speech (or discourse) is the actual use of this system in some concrete circumstance.

Speech act theory. A **contemporary** philosophical approach to language inspired by J. L. **Austin's** *How to Do Things with Words* (1962) and advanced by John Searle in *Speech Acts* (1969). Austin challenged the deep-seated tendency to suppose that the only or main **function** of language is the utterance of statements purporting to describe the world. Any adequate account of human language must recognize that, in addition to **constative** utterances (statements about which it makes sense to ask if they are true or false), there are **performative** utterances (for example, taking a vow, making a promise, or issuing a threat). Austin also discovered that one and the same utterance might have a **locutionary force,** an **illocutionary force,** and a **perlocutionary force.**

Stare pro. Latin meaning "to stand for." From ancient to contemporary times, the function of one thing standing for another has been taken to define what a sign is (see *aliquid stat pro aliquo*).

In one of the most famous texts in the history of semiotics, Aristotle can be interpreted to be claiming that spoken signs stand for mental signs and written signs stand for spoken signs. Our impressions and ideas are themselves signs: They stand for things outside the soul (or, in more modern parlance, for things independent of the mind). Aristotle presumes that, though we might speak and thus write in different languages, we nonetheless form the same ideas and (by means of these ideas) know the same world. Especially in recent times, this presumption has been strenuously challenged. See also **Sapir–Whorf hypothesis.**

Stoic theory of signs. An important doctrine in an early phase of semiotic inquiry or reflection. One crucial part of this doctrine is the contention that a sign links together three components: (1) the material and thus perceptible sign vehicle (for example, a sound or inscription), (2) the meaning or lekton (that which is meant or said), and (3) an external object. Here we clearly have a **triadic** model of the sign. The Stoic theory of the sign was a basic part of Stoic logic, a highly developed doctrine still worthy of careful study. In opposition to making an immaterial entity (the lekton) a part of the sign, Epicurean philosophers proposed a **dyadic** model of the sign in which only sensory impressions and material objects were granted status.

Story/plot. Story, the term ordinarily used to translate the Russian word *fabula*; plot, the word used to translate *sjuzet*. The Russian formalists drew an important distinction between story and plot. The story is the pre-literary sequence of events providing the writer with raw material, whereas the plot is the literary reordering of this sequence. According to the Russian formalists, the function of the plot is to make strange the sequence of events (see **defamiliarization**).

"Strange, making." Translation of Russian *ostranenie*. See also **defamiliarization.**

Structural linguistics. The study of **language** based on the principles of **structuralism.**

Structuralism, structuralist. A metatheory regarding the construction of theories. Structuralism has appeared in the twentieth century as a theory of, for example, mind, language, culture, and literature. Beyond these specific structuralist theories, there is an at least implicit theory of how all theories ought to be constructed or undertaken. Just as the term **metalanguage** is the name for a language used to talk about language, so **metatheory** is the name for a theory of theories. As a metatheory, structuralism insists upon the necessity to conceive any object of inquiry as a structure. According to Jean Piaget, "the notion of structure is comprised of three key ideas: the idea of wholeness, the idea of transformation, and the idea of self-regulation" (1968 [1970], 5). A whole is more than an aggregate: While an aggregate is a random or unintegrated collection of items, a **system** is a structure exhibiting a high degree of both regularity (the opposite of randomness) and integration. A pile of leaves is an aggregate, the child hiding under the pile is a system. An economic system entails various forms of transformation—for example, how to transform labor into capital, or capital into more capital; a linguistic system also entails possibilities for transformations of various sorts—how to transform words into sentences, sentences into one another, etc. Finally, the functioning of systems is not explained primarily in terms of external factors (that is, factors outside of the system). Systems are structures manifesting an *inherent* dynamic: They are self-moving and self-regulating structures. (Think here of a living organism.)

Ferdinand de **Saussure**'s conception of **language** (*langue*) as a system to be studied synchronically was crucial, to say the least, in the development of structuralism. But, as many of the most basic assumptions of structuralism began to be challenged (for example, the possibility, let alone the desirability, of separating **diachronic** considerations from synchronic ones; the autonomy of systems vis-á-vis outside factors), a new metatheory has emerged—**poststructuralism.** But, because this new orientation is so deeply suspicious of just those things structuralism cherished (scienticity and, more generally, the possibility of weaving theoretical nets both large enough and with narrow enough mesh to catch the essence of, say, a language or a culture), it is best not to refer to poststructuralism as a metatheory. Any doctrine so suspicious of and, in some cases, hostile to theory—especially grand theory—is mispresented by the designation *metatheory*; perhaps a better word here is *sensibility.* See also **hermeneutics of suspicion, synchronic.**

Subject, subjectivity. A good way to get at the meaning of this term is to view it as the mirror image of René **Descartes**'s *cogito.* When Descartes triumphantly declares against the **skeptic** in his *Meditations on First Philosophy, Cogito ergo sum* ("I think, therefore I am"), the "I" who makes this declaration has cast into doubt his own body and the world around him. He has also ignored the importance of language as an instrument of thought (see **dialogism** and **thought**), not merely of communication. Finally, he identifies this "I" as a thinking self and this thinking being as a consciousness fully or largely transparent to itself. As ordinarily used today, subjectivity is the name for the "I" when conceived as an *embodied* and *situated* self, whose ability to think depends on language and whose awareness of itself is distorted as well as partial.

Subject is often used to call attention to other characteristics of the "I," ones highlighted for the sake of challenging more traditional images of the human person. Above all, the *embedded* subject (the "I" as it is actually embedded in a historical setting and cultural system) is only problematically an *autonomous* self: The cultural overdetermination of human action is stressed to the point of calling into question human freedom (or autonomy). Connected with this, *subject* is used to underscore our fate as beings subjected to historical and cultural forces and structures. Finally, the reflexivity of the subject is, as in more traditional views, taken to be crucial. There is, however, a difference as well: In contemporary semiotic and **poststructuralist** writings on subjectivity, there is a deep sensitivity to the fact that the ways we refer to and represent ourselves are intricately (though not obviously) tied to the ways others refer to and represent us.

After Freud, it is difficult to be unconscious of the unconscious. Descartes, however, did not have the benefit of Freud's theories, having been born several centuries before. The unity and transparency of the *cogito* (the "I" as conceived by Descartes) is replaced by a subject *divided in itself* (consciousness/unconscious) and, to a significant degree, *opaque to itself.* See also **decentering of the subject.**

Subjectivity, Primacy of. The assumption or position that we start inside our own consciousness or subjectivity. The meanings of words, for example, is first and foremost the images and ideas that float through one's consciousness when one hears these words. This assumption is untenable; for it in effect denies the very possibility of communication. If what you mean is what floats through your mind, and if your mind is for me and everyone else a black box (a domain accessible only to you), then what you mean is, in principle, inaccessible to me and all others. To assert the primacy of subjectivity amounts to nothing less than endorsing the image of our minds as hermetically sealed territories. There is nothing gained—indeed, there is much lost—by denying the private or inward dimensions of human experience and consciousness. But the very prefix of the word consciousness suggests that we do not begin shut up in a closet: We begin *with* others. To discover what our words mean and even what our feelings are, others are essential. See also **intersubjectivity, dialogism, private language, usage.**

Sujet en proces. French expression used by Julia **Kristeva** and others to designate the **subject** in process/on trial.

Suture. A term meaning, in general, the process of joining together two edges or surfaces and, in the semiotics of film, designating the basic cinematic technique of joining different shots together to construct a narrative. Sometimes this term is used more narrowly to refer to a specific type of cinematic technique (for example, the shot/reverse shot). For an informative discussion of suture, see Kaja Silverman's *The Subject of Semiotics* (1983).

Symbol. A term frequently used to designate a **conventional sign** (for instance, a sign based on **convention** or established **usage**). But this term refers to various other types of signs as well. For Ferdinand de **Saussure,** a symbol is a sign in which the correlation between **signifier** and **signified** is, in some measure, motivated (that is, nonarbitrary). In Charles **Peirce**'s elaborate classification of signs, a symbol is almost the opposite of this. Peirce defines symbol as part of a **trichotomy: icon, index, symbol.** This trichotomy is based on the relationship between the **sign vehicle** and its **object.** If a sign vehicle is related to its object by virtue of a resemblance to that object (for instance, a map to its territory), it is an icon. If it is related to its object by virtue of an actual or physical connection (for example, the direction of the weathervane to the direction of the wind being indicated by the vane), it is an index. If it is related to its object by virtue of a habit or convention (for instance a single red rose as the symbol of affection—or more), it is a symbol.

Yet another important meaning of symbol is that it is a

sign that partakes of the very thing or person it symbolizes. Still another is a sign calling for open-ended interpretation—a sign infinitely rich in significance.

Symbolic order or **register.** An expression used by Jacques **Lacan,** Julia **Kristeva,** and numerous other contributors to **semiotics** to designate the social order as a symbolic arena into which human beings are initiated and in which they are destined to act. As a result of such initiation and participation, the symbolic becomes internalized; thus it is not only an arena in which subjects are situated but also a dimension of their very subjectivity. The most important institutions making up this order are language, morality, law, and religion. It is only by being subjected to the constraints and inhibitions of the symbolic order that human subjectivity is engendered. For psychoanalytically oriented semioticians such as Lacan and Kristeva, the initiation into the symbolic order is tied to the Oedipal conflict. See also **imaginary, Real, engendering of subjectivity.**

Synchronic vs. **diachronic.** Synchronic, pertaining to that which is co-present or simultaneous or that for which the passage of time is considered irrelevant; diachronic, pertaining to what changes over time. Imagine that at this moment the Congress of the United States is in session. We might investigate this fact in light of the history leading up to it; or we might abstract from this history and consider the goings-on of Congress at this moment (the word "abstraction" is derived from two Greek words meaning to draw away from. A *diachronic* study examines its object in light of its history, as something moving across or through time. In contrast, a *synchronic* investigation considers its object as a **system** operating or functioning in the present. A diachronic examination draws us *toward* history, the process in which differences unfold successively; a synchronic consideration draws us *away from* history, toward some system in which differences are simultaneously at work. To return to our example: Think of the different forms of government leading up to our present-day Congress; then think of the different forces simultaneously jockeying for position during the present session of Congress. The first is diachronic, the second synchronic. See also **diachronic.**

Synechdoche. A **trope** or figure of speech in which a part of something is used to designate or symbolize the whole (for example, when basketball players say that they're going to play hoops) or just the opposite—in which the whole is used to designate a part.

Synechism. A term Charles S. **Peirce** coined to designate the doctrine of **continuity.**

Syntactics. A term used by Charles **Morris** to designate that branch of **semiotics** concerned with the relationship between a **sign vehicle** and other sign vehicles.

Syntagm. Any combination of units (for example, words) that makes sense. A sentence is an example of a syntagm.

Syntagmatic vs. **paradigmatic.** See **associative, axis.**

System. Any structure characterized by a high degree of regularity and integration. In this sense, a living organism is a biological system. See also **structuralism.**

T

Taxonomy. A classification; the study of the principles of classification. Charles S. **Peirce** was interested in taxonomy in both of these senses. Also, he and Ferdinand de **Saussure** (the co-founders of contemporary **semiotics**) both devoted attention to the classification of the sciences. For Peirce, semiotics was one of three **normative sciences** (**ethics** and **aesthetics** are the other two) which were part of philosophy. For Saussure, *semiologie* (his name for the general theory of signs) would be, when it came into existence, a branch of social psychology. The different way Peirce and Saussure conceive the relation of sign theory to other areas of investigation is only one of numerous important differences in their approaches to this theory. See also **typology.**

Text. A term used today in a very broad sense to cover not only **verbal** but also other forms of communication. One might encounter the claim that a face, or a city, is a text. A distinctive feature of this newly emerged use of *text* is that the derivation of this word from the Latin *texere* ("to weave") and textum ("a web; texture") appears to inform the use. The text is something woven; but now readers join authors or writers as the weavers of texts. That is, the emphasis is on the text as an open and perhaps even unfinished process. For deconstructionists, the traditional assumption of literary criticism that the text should be approached as a coherent whole is rejected. Texts deconstruct themselves: They unravel. A good reader will be able to discover those points at which a text comes apart. But, in order to discover this, readers must read "from the margins"—that is, be attentive to seemingly marginal or peripheral concerns found in a text. It is important to stress that deconstruction—the process of a text unraveling—results not from the exertion of external pressure or force, but from inherent features of the text itself. "The movements of deconstruction do not," Derrida contends, "destroy structures [for example, texts] from outside. They are not possible and effective, nor can they take accurate aim, except by inhabiting those structures [or texts]" (24). Deconstructive criticism is an *immanent* critique. This means that the deconstructionist reader or critic is always complicit. No one is innocent: We are all champions of what we oppose—even if our advocacy of, or support for, our own enemies escapes us. Part of deconstruction's challenge is to foster an awareness of how deeply intertwined we are with the very things we oppose. There is no neutral ground, no innocent party. Even the most committed critics of patriarchy (that is, rule by, or dominance of, males) are always, in some measure, unwitting advocates of patriarchy. The **critique** of patriarchy is aided by acknowledging this. A central concern of deconstructionism is, in part, to stress the need to acknowledge one's complicity with one's opponents in this and other contexts.

Thematize. Make explicit and focal.

Thirdness. One of Charles S. **Peirce's** three universal **categories.** Formally and abstractly defined, it is betweenness or **mediation** (CP 5.104). Everything is something in itself; this Peirce calls **firstness.** We might call this initselfness. Everything either actually or potentially reacts against, or opposes itself, to other things; this he calls **secondness** (over-againstness). Everything is, in some measure, intelligible, if only because it can be related by me to something else. For example, I unexpectedly receive some flowers. My first reaction is to say "What's this?" Something is, as it were, thrown in my way or thrust upon me: The bunch of flowers confronts me as an **object** (*ob-*, against; *jacere,* to throw). It arrests my attention; but, then, I take these flowers to mean someone is thinking of me. The flowers project my thought to something other than themselves. I see them as a link between myself and some other person. Finally, I am drawn to the beauty and color of these flowers; I become absorbed in the flowers themselves, in what they are in themselves—an absorption so complete that it is like a dream (a state of consciousness in which there is neither a sharp distinction between myself and my world—in fact, I'm oblivious to my surroundings—nor any self-conscious struggle to make sense out of what is before me). Let's now retrace our steps quickly: The flowers confront me initially in their otherness or secondness ("What's this?"), then are rendered intelligible by being related to something other than themselves or me ("Someone is thinking of me"); finally, they so completely absorb my attention that all else fades away but what they uniquely and qualitatively are. The bare bones of this simple narrative might be described thus: Againstness (secondness or opposition) is followed by in-betweenness (thirdness or mediation), and in-betweenness is followed by in-itselfness (firstness or immediacy).

One of Peirce's own favorite examples of thirdness or mediation is an act of giving. For him, giving exhibits an irreducibly triadic structure or form—that is, any attempt to break it down into a simpler affair loses its meaning. In any act of giving, there is a giver, a recipient, and a gift. One half of this act is divestiture (the giver divests herself of something she owns); the other half is appropriation (the recipient appropriates or comes to own something new). But, in giving, these two dyads (giver and gift-as-divested; recipient and gift-as-acquired) are integrally united. If the giver simply gets rid of her property and, a little while later, the recipient comes along and finds it, we have two accidentally related dyads but no act of giving. In formulating his three categories and, in partic-ular, his category of thirdness, Peirce was not trying to be needlessly abstruse or difficult. But he was trying to counter our deeply ingrained tendency to conceive things too simply.

Thought. The process or act of thinking; the product or result of this process or act. In semiotics, thought is conceived as a sign process.

To its advocates, **semiotics** entails a conceptual revolution, a radical revision in the way we think about such things as **mind, consciousness,** thoughts, and even feeling. Charles S. **Peirce** suggested: "There is no reason why 'thought' . . . should be taken in that narrow sense in which silence and darkness are favorable to thought. It should rather be understood as covering all rational life, so that an experiment shall be an operation of thought" (CP 5.420). Especially in the **modern** period of Western thought, the tendency to conceive thought as a process taking place inside one's mind or head has been pronounced. This, in effect, makes privacy ("silence and darkness") an essential feature of thought. For Peirce and other semioticians, this is a mistake. That we often retreat to the theater of the imagination to perform ideal experiments is undeniable; that such private or hidden experiments are the original, only, or most important form of thinking is highly doubtful.

In sum, though there is no consensus among semioticians, there is a pronounced tendency to construe thought as a process of **dialogue,** sometimes taking place in the private sphere or in our imaginations, but often (perhaps even most often) taking place in the public arena of our worldly engagements and entanglements.

According to Peirce, it is of the very essence of thought to be specific, just as it is of its essence to be general. Thought simultaneously drives in opposite directions—toward specific applications and toward ever higher generalities (CP 5.594-5). In other words, thought is a dialectical process. The field of semiotics reveals just this aspect of thought, for it exhibits a drive to become acquainted, on the one hand, with the specific varieties and applications of signs and, on the other, with signs in general. The one side is clearly seen in the elaborate classifications of signs devised by semioticians, the other in the general definitions or models of signs (or **semiosis**) found in their writings. See also **tuism**.

Token vs. **type**. See **type** vs. **token**.

Trace. A term occupying an important place in Jacques **Derrida**'s **grammatology**. Trace or inscription has the place in Derrida's grammatology that sign has in Ferdinand de **Saussure**'s *semiologie* and in Charles S. **Peirce**'s *semeiotic*. If a thing never left a *trace* of itself it could never be known, nor could it serve as a sign of anything else. Thus, without visible or tangible or, in some other way, perceptible marks or traces, **semiosis** (or sign action) would be impossible. But without space or spacing, semiosis would also be impossible: If none of the words on this page were spaced apart, there would be a blot of ink, but no words (or graphic signs). If something could be fully and everlastingly present (see **presence**), it would not need to leave a trace of itself: Since it would always be around, it would not need to leave messages that it was here or that it will be there. Such messages are, after all, what traces convey. I see footprints outside my apartment and infer someone *was* here; I see clouds and infer it *will* rain. The trace is tied to what is *not* present, for example, what is no longer here or what is not yet here. For Derrida, it is tied to what could never, in principle, be present. There is an ancient, powerful, and persistent dream that the traces we encounter in the texts of nature and humanity can lead to face-to-face encounters in which self and

197

other are fully present to one another; the dream that the traces are, as it were, a ladder which we can use to climb up a ridge and, after reaching the ridge, kick away. If presence is possible, signs—or traces—are dispensable: At some point, we can discard them, for they are no longer needed. We shall see face-to-face, without the intermediary of signs, God, or Nature, or whatever other name we might use for what can be absolutely (that is, fully and finally) present.

Derrida's deconstructionism highlights traces, spaces, differences, etc. as a way of trying to awaken us from this ancient, powerful, and persistent dream. See also **transcendental signified.**

Transcendental. A term introduced by Immanuel Kant and widely used by philosophers to designate a form of inquiry or reflection sharply distinguished from empirical and experimental modes of investigation. A transcendental investigation is concerned with exploring the conditions for the possibility of whatever is being investigated. Sometimes **semiotics** is said to be transcendental in just this Kantian sense, for it inquires into the conditions for the possibility of meaning (or communicating).

Transcendental signified. An expression used by Jacques **Derrida** and other deconstructionists to designate any **signified** that is allegedly not itself a **signifier.** Appeals to any transcendental signified have the effect, in the judgment of deconstructionists, of arresting (as the thought police might arrest) the **play** of signifiers. For Derrida, there is no transcendental signified, for all signifieds turn out, in one way or another, to become caught up in the play of signifiers. His opposition to the notion of a transcendental signified is central to his **critique** of **presence.** For the transcendental signified is supposed to be what is fully and finally present, or (put differently) what is absolute and immediately present. See also **trace.**

Transuasion. One of Charles S. **Peirce's** names for **thirdness.**

Triadic. Three-termed; having three parts, aspects or levels. Charles S. **Peirce's** definition of **sign** as a correlation of **sign vehicle, object, interpretant** is described as triadic, whereas Ferdinand de **Saussure's** definition of sign as a correlation between **signifier** and **signified** is characterized as **dyadic** (two-termed).

Trichotomy. While a **dichotomy** is the process of dividing something into two, or the result of this process, a trichotomy is the process of dividing something into three, or the result of this process (a threefold division or classification). Ferdinand de **Saussure's** approach to the study of signs tends to be dichotomous, whereas Charles S. **Peirce's** tends to be trichotomous or **triadic.**

Trope. A figure of speech; a word or expression used in a figurative (rather than a literal) sense. **Metaphor, metonymy,** and **synecdoche** are among the most common tropes. *Metaphor* is sometimes used in a very broad sense as a synonym for trope (that is, as a term covering all figures of speech). It is also used more narrowly to designate a specific figure of speech.

The identification and analysis of the most important tropes were central concerns of classical rhetoric. In this and other respects, classical rhetoric is of value to contemporary semioticians. Here, as in so many other contexts (for example logic and linguistics), the investigation of signs has been undertaken, though not under the name of semiotics nor with the conscious aim of articulating a general theory.

Tuism. A term coined by Charles S. **Peirce** to designate a distinctive conception of thought. One cannot improve upon his own definition: "The doctrine that all **thought** is addressed to a second person, or to one's future self as to a second person" (W 1:xxix). See also **dialogism.**

Tychism. A term coined by Charles S. **Peirce** to designate the doctrine of absolute or objective chance.

Type vs. **token.** Type, a sign considered as an indefinitely replicable entity or function; token, an individual replication or instance of a sign or, more exactly, of a **legisign.** The type is itself the legisign, a form indefinitely replicable. There can be numerous tokens of a single type. For example, the word "the" appears countless times in this glossary and indeed in numerous other writings. In one sense, the same word is appearing in different places. But the different instances or instantiations are just that: different. This "the" is different from all other instances. Peirce marks this distinction by calling these instances or instantiations tokens of the type "the." When we say that the *same* word is found in countless places, we mean the type; when we say that there are 59,049 instances of it in a particular tome, we mean the token. Since types are replicated in tokens, Peirce sometimes used **replica** as a synonym for token. Joseph Ransdell has suggested that type and token are best seen as part of a triad—tone, token, type—and that this triad is equivalent to the trichotomy of **qualisign, sinsign, legisign.**

Typology. A synonym for classification (see **taxonomy**). The writings of semioticians abound in typologies of signs. The simplest of these is perhaps the classification of signs as natural and **conventional,** the most complex undoubtedly Charles S. **Peirce**'s suggestion (arrived at through a mathematical formula) that there are 59,049 kinds of sign (CP 1.291).

U

Umwelt. German word usually translated "surrounding world" or, more simply, "environment." Jakob von Uexkull, a biologist whose work bears directly upon **semiotics,** used this term to designate the environment insofar as an organism is equipped to perceive it. Accordingly, the *Umwelt* is not simply what is objectively there, but only what is perceptually and operationally available to the organism.

Universal. A term predicable of numerous or even countless individuals (for example, *human being*). From as far back as the ancient Greek philosopher Plato to **contemporary** authors, the status of universals has been a topic of controversy. See also **general, nominalism, realism.**

Unmotivated. Synonym for **arbitrary;** lacking an intrinsic connection or natural basis. According to Ferdinand de **Saussure** and the countless structuralists and semioticians whom he influenced, a **sign** comes into being on the basis of an arbitrary correlation between, say, a sound and a concept. This correlation is also called unmotivated: There is nothing in the sound image itself that links it to its correlative concept. The **phoneme** "boy" bears no resemblance to its **sememe** (meaning). Saussure did acknowledge that some signs—for example, a pair of scales as a symbol of justice—are motivated. But he minimized the importance of such signs.

Usage/use. The way language is customarily or ordinarily used, with the implication that such usage is more or less authoritative. Lugwig **Wittgenstein** in his later thought is reported to have advised: "Don't ask for the meaning of a word; look to its *use.*" It is only, or primarily, by attending to the actual and various ways in which words and statements are used that we learn what words mean. **Meaning** is not to be sought either in some private sphere (for example, one's own mind or consciousness) or in some transcendent realm (Plato's Forms or "Ideas"); it is to be sought in the established usages of ordinary language. Wittgenstein did not intend this as a "theory" of meaning; in fact, he was deeply suspicious of all such theories. They are part of the problem. The solution is to turn with painstaking care to ordinary usage. This approach to meaning was near, or even at, the center of the **linguistic turn** in contemporary Anglo-American philosophy.

Utterer. A term used by Charles S. **Peirce** and others to designate the producer of signs (for example, a graph, **text,** or **discourse**). An utterer, thus, should not be conceived necessarily as a speaker in the ordinary sense; it means something far more general. See also **addresser.**

V

Value. In its most familiar sense, the *value* of anything is its worth. But, in Ferdinand de **Saussure**'s **linguistics,** value (*valeur*) means something quite different and, in fact, difficult. *Value* is a term borrowed from economics because Saussure was consciously trying to develop a comparison between economics and his own approach to linguistics. Since diachronic linguistics studies the development or evolution of language, it corresponds to economic history; and since synchronic linguistics investigates the formal mechanisms operative within a given linguistic system, it corresponds to what was called in Saussure's day "political economics" and in our own simply "economics." In linguistics no less than in economics "we are confronted with the notion of *value;* both sciences are concerned with *a system for equating things of different orders*—labor and wages in one and a signified and signifier in the other."

Verbal. From *verbum,* Latin for "word." Related to or consisting of words; for example, verbal communication is communication by means of words.

Verbicide. The killing of a word. Words are sometimes used in such careless and sloppy ways that they lose their distinctive meaning. For example, "awful" has been effectively murdered: One cannot use it to designate something inspiring awe, for its looser senses (awful as a synonym for terrible or objectionable) have become virtually its only senses—despite what many dictionaries identify as its first meanings.

Verbum mentis. Latin expression meaning mental (or inner) word. In **medieval** thought, it was often supposed that, prior to and independent of words in their ordinary, public sense, there are inner or mental words. These mental words are pre- or extralinguistic concepts. To suppose that there are such words would make thought more independent of language and symbolization than almost all contemporary semioticians would grant.

Verifiability. From Latin *veritas,* truth. The capacity of a statement to be verified (or proven true). *Verifiability* was the watchword of positivists. They tried to use the criterion of verifiability as a way of distinguishing meaningful from meaningless assertions or statements. For them, if a statement is, in principle, verifiable (that is, if there is some evidence or experience that could establish its truth), then the statement is meaningful; if, however, a statement is in principle unverifiable, then it is meaningless. The fate of positivism was tied to the principle of verifiability. When this principle was discredited—at least, in the crude and reductionistic sense in which it was often wielded by positivists—so too was positivism.

Verstehen. See **Erklarung.**

W

Welby, Victoria Lady (1837–1912). Around the same time that Ferdinand de **Saussure** announced the possibility of *semiologie* (a science devoted to investigating "the life of signs in society"), Lady Victoria Welby conceived *significs*, "the study of the nature of significance in all its forms and relations" (1911: vii). Her two major works are *What Is Meaning?* (1903) and *Significs and Language* (1911). Charles S. **Peirce** favorably reviewed the earlier book after Welby took the initiative by requesting her publisher to send him a copy. At this time, she also initiated their correspondence, which lasted until shortly before her death. This exchange of letters, available in *Semiotic and Significs* (Bloomington: Indiana University Press, 1977), a book edited by Charles S. Hardwick, contains important and seminal ideas regarding the nature and varieties of signs. Though today Welby is better known for her correspondence with Peirce than for her own writings, these have a value perhaps yet to be fully appreciated.

Weltanschuuang. German for "world-view" or "philosophy of life."

Wittgenstein, Ludwig Josef Johann (1889–1951). One of the most influential twentieth-century philosophers. Born into a wealthy Austrian family, he eventually secured a position teaching philosophy at Cambridge. Since he came to repudiate many of his early views, a distinction is made between the early and the later Wittgenstein. His early views are found in *Tractatus Logico-Philosophicus* (1922), while his mature position is presented in *Philosophical Investigations* (1953), published posthumously. Initially, more through his personal encounters as a teacher and colleague than through his writings, Wittgenstein exerted an enormous influence on Anglo-American philosophy. The linguistic turn owed much to his thought, early and later. His critique of **private language,** his construal of **meaning** as **usage,** his notions of **language-games, form of life,** and **philosophy** as a form of conceptual therapy all have direct and deep relevance to the study of signs.

Writable or **writerly text.** Two ways of translating Roland **Barthes**'s term *scriptible*, a term used to distinguish a distinctive type of literary text. In contrast to readerly (*lisible*) texts, writerly texts are ones in which the reader is invited to engage self-consciously in the construction or fabrication of the text's meaning. Such texts are characteristically challenging: They try in various ways to jar their readers by exposing, rather than hiding, the devices and codes by which narratives are constructed. Think here of James Joyce's *Ulysses* or *Finnegan's Wake*, certainly paradigms of writerly texts. While a readerly text is presented as a finished product to be consumed, the writerly text is designed as an ongoing process to be joined. Writerly texts are intended to be subversive, to challenge the dominant ethos of bourgeois society. For this ethos (at least in the judgment of Barthes and numerous other cultural critics) turns everything (including texts or writings) into a commodity and many commodities into fetishes. These texts are too challenging to allow their readers the pleasure of passive consumption. See also **bliss, text of.**

Writing. The process of inscribing signs in a more or less durable medium; the result of this process—in a word, inscription. Traditionally, it has been supposed that writing is a secondary system of signs, written words being themselves signs of spoken signs. In recent decades, however, this privileging of speech has been challenged by the deconstructionist Jacques **Derrida.** *Ecriture* (the French word for writing) is conceived as the primordial play of formal differences by which signs and thus meanings are generated. It should not be assumed that writing in this sense can be identified with writing in its ordinary sense, though there are similarities that Derrida wants to exploit (for example, the materiality of signs).

The very words **language** and linguistics (the study of language) both derive from *lingua* (Latin for "tongue") and, thus, point to speaking rather than writing. Leonard Bloomfield, an influential linguist, even claimed that "writing is not language, but merely a way of recording language by means of visible marks" (1933, 21). This claim in effect echoes Ferdinand de **Saussure**'s position: "Language and writing are two distinct systems of signs; the second exists for the sole purpose of representing the first. The linguistic object is not both the written and the spoken forms of words; the spoken forms along constitute the object [of linguistics]" (1916 [1966], 23–4). Language is here conceived as a formal **system** of auditory **signs.**

This view of language has been recently characterized as **phonocentric** (from Greek *phonema,* speech), since it focuses primarily or exclusively on linguistic signs as sound images or aural forms. Jacques **Derrida**'s **grammatology,** "a science of writing before and in speech," is designed to challenge the phonocentric bias of semiotic investigation. For Derrida, writing "signifies inscription and especially the durable institution of a sign" (1967, 44). So understood, writing (often called **arche-writing**) becomes nothing less than an equivalent of **semiosis,** or sign action. In our discourses about signs, the instituted or inscribed **trace,** the "written" and durable mark—rather than the sound image—needs to be made the focal concern. Such, at least, is a central claim of Derrida's grammatology.

Writing under erasure. See **erasure.**

"Writing degree zero." See **zero degree.**

Z

Zeichen. German for **sign;** also symbol, mark, token; badge; **signal,** indication, evidence.

Zeichentheorie. German for sign theory, thus a synonym for **semiotics.**

Zeitgeist. German word meaning spirit of the times or the age. It is ordinarily used to designate the prevailing sensibility or mood of an epoch.

Zero Degree. Roland **Barthes**'s term for a style of writing that tries to efface or hide itself. In writers such as Emile Zola, Albert Camus, and Ernest Hemingway we encounter a style that is carefully crafted not to call attention to itself. Quickly (if not immediately), however, such a "zero degree" or "absence" of style is seen for what it is—a distinctive or unique style.

Zoosemiosis. The whole range of sign processes found in the world of animals. Sometimes zoosemiosis is used in a broad sense, inclusive of **anthroposemiosis,** and at other times it is used in a narrower sense excluding the sign processes and sign forms unique to human beings (Homo sapiens).

Zoosemiotics. The branch of **semiotics** devoted to **zoosemiosis.** This term was coined by Thomas **Sebeok** in 1963 and defined then as "the discipline, within which the science of signs intersects with ethology, devoted to the scientific study of signaling behavior in and across animal species" (1972, 178). Ethology is the scientific study of animal behavior, while ethnology is that branch of anthropology devoted to investigating socioeconomic systems and cultural traditions, especially in those societies without modern technologies. Both fields of study intersect with semiotics in numerous and important ways.

Selected Bibliography

Austin, J. L. *Philosophical Papers*. Oxford: Oxford University Press, 1961.

Barthes, Roland. *Elements of Semiology*. New York: Hill & Wang, 1967.

_____. *The Fashion System*. New York: Hill & Wang, 1983.

_____. *A Barthes Reader*, ed. by Susan Sontag. New York: Hill & Wang, 1982.

_____. *Image-Music-Text*. New York: Hill & Wang, 1977.

_____. *Pleasure of the Text*. New York: Hill & Wang, 1976.

_____. *S/Z*. New York: Hill & Wang, 1974.

Cassirer, Ernst. *The Philosophy of Symbolic Forms*, 3 vols. New Haven, Conn.: Yale University Press, 1957.

Clarke, D. S. *Principles of Semiotic*. London: Routledge & Kegan Paul, 1987.

Culler, Jonathan. *On Deconstruction*. London: Routledge & Kegan Paul, 1983.

_____. *The Pursuit of Signs*. Ithaca, N.Y.: Cornell University Press, 1983.

————. *Ferdinand de Saussere*, rev. ed. Ithaca, N.Y.: Cornell University Press, 1986.

Deely, John. *Basics of Semiotics*. Bloomington: Indiana University Press, 1990.

————. *Introducing Semiotics: Its History and Doctrine*. Bloomington: Indiana University Press, 1982.

Derrida, Jacques. *Dissemination*. Chicago: University of Chicago Press, 1981.

————. *Margins of Philosophy*. Chicago: University of Chicago Press, 1982.

————. *Of Grammatology*. Chicago: University of Chicago, 1976.

————. *Writing and Difference*. Chicago: University of Chicago Press, 1978.

Dewey, John. *On Experience, Nature and Freedom*, ed. by Richard J. Bernstein. Indianapolis: Library of Liberal Arts, 1960.

Eagleton, Terry. *Literary Theory: An Introduction*. Minneapolis: University of Minnesota Press, 1983.

Eco, Umberto. *The Role of the Reader*. Bloomington: Indiana University Press, 1979.

————. *A Theory of Semiotics*. Bloomington: Indiana University Press, 1976.

Fisch, Max H. *Peirce, Semiotic, and Pragmatism*. ed. by Kenneth Laine Ketner and Christian J. W. Kloesel. Bloomington: Indiana University Press.

Foucault, Michel. *Language, Counter-Memory, Practice: Selected Essays and Interviews*. Ithaca, N.Y.: Cornell University Press, 1977.

————. *The Order of Things: An Archeology of the Human Sciences*. New York: Random House, 1970.

Gadamer, Hans-Georg. *Philosophical Hermeneutics*. Berkeley: University of California Press.

Greimas, A. J. *Structural Semnataics*. Lincoln: University of Nebraska Press, 1983.

Greimas, A. J., and Joseph Courtés. *Semiotics and Language: An Analytical Dictionary*. Bloomington: Indiana University Press, 1982.

Hawkes, Terrence. *Structuralism and Semiotics*. Berkeley: University of California Press, 1977.

Hjelmslev, Louis. *Prolegomena to a Theory of Language*. Madison: University of Wisconsin Press, 1974.

Hoy, David Couzens. *The Critical Circle: Literature, History, and Philosophical Hermeneutics*. Berkeley: University of California Press, 1978.

Jakobson, Roman. *Verbal Art, Verbal Sign, Verbal Time*. Minneapolis: University of Minnesota Press, 1985.

Jameson, Frederic. *The Prison-House of Language: A Critical Account of Structuralism and Russian Formalism*. Princeton, N.J.: Princeton University Press, 1972.

Kristeva, Julia. *Desire in Language*, ed. by L. Roudiez (NY: Columbia University Press, 1980).

———. *The Kristeva Reader*, ed. by Toril Moi (Oxford: Blackwell, 1986).

Lyotard, Jean-Francois. *The Postmodern Condition-A Report on Knowledge*. Minneapolis: University of Minnesota, 1984.

Noth, Winfred. *Handbook of Semiotics*. Bloomington: Indiana University Press, 1990.

Piaget, Jean. *Structuralism*. New York: Harper, 1971.

Peirce, Charles Sanders. *Collected Papers*, vols. 1–6 edited by Charles Hartshorne and Paul Weiss; vols. 7 and 8 edited by Arthur W. Burks. Cambridge, Mass.: Harvard University Press, 1931–1958.

———. *Semiotic and Significs: The Correspondence between Charles S. Peirce and Victoria Lady Welby*, edited by Charles S. Hardwick. Bloomington: Indiana University Press, 1977.

Sarup, Madan. *An Introduction to Post Structuralism and Postmodernism*. Athens: University of Georgia Press, 1989.

Saussure, Ferdinand de. *Course in General Linguistics*, translated by Wade Baskin. New York: McGraw-Hill, 1969.

Savan, David. *An Introduction to C. S. Peirce's Full System of Semeiotic*. Toronto: Toronto Semiotic Circle, 1987–1988.

Sebeok, Thomas. *Contributions to the Doctrine of Signs*. Lanham, Md.: University Press of America, 1985.

_____. *The Sign and Its Masters*. Austin: University of Texas Press, 1979.

_____, (ed.). *Encyclopedic Dictionary of Semiotics*, 3 vols. Berlin: Mouton de Gruyter, 1986.

Sheriff, John K. *The Fate of Meaning: Charles Peirce, Structuralism, and Literature*. Princeton, N.J.: Princeton University Press, 1989.

Silverman, Kaja. *The Subject of Semiotics*. New York: Oxford University Press, 1983.

Smith, Paul. *Discerning the Subject*. Minneapolis: University of Minnesota Press, 1988.

Wittgenstein, Ludwig. *Philosophical Investigations*. Oxford: Blackwell, 1953.

Woolf, Virgina. *A Room of One's Own*. New York: Harcourt Brace Jovanovich, 1957.

212

About the Author

Vincent M. Colapietro, associate professor of philosophy at Fordham University, is a scholar recognized for his contributions to two overlapping fields of research: American philosophy and semiotics. He is the author of *Peirce's Approach to the Self: A Semiotic Perspective on Human Subjectivity* (1989) and articles on Peirce, James, Dewey, and other figures in American thought. In other writings he has examined and evaluated, from the perspective of a Peircean pragmatism, the views of such thinkers as Ferdinand de Saussure, Umberto Eco, Richard Rorty, and Jacques Derrida.

He is a consulting editor to the *Transactions of the Charles S. Peirce Society* and an active member in both the Semiotic Society of America and the Society for the Advancement of American Philosophy.